lonely 🌏 planet P9-ECJ-203

POCKET

LOS ANGELES

TOP EXPERIENCES • LOCAL LIFE

CRISTIAN BONETTO, ANDREW BENDER

Contents

Plan Your Trip 4

Street entertainer, Hollywood Blvd (p36)
VALERIYA ZANKOVYCH/SHUTTERSTOCK ©

COVID-19

We have re-checked every business in this book before publication to ensure that it is still open after the COVID-19 outbreak. However, the economic and social impacts of COVID-19 will continue to be felt long after the outbreak has been contained, and many businesses, services and events referenced in this guide may experience ongoing restrictions. Some businesses may be temporarily closed, have changed their opening hours and services, or require bookings; some unfortunately could have closed permanently. We suggest you check with venues before visiting for the latest information.

Los Angeles' Top Experiences

Go star-spotting on Hollywood's Walk of Fame (p36)

ARKANTO/SHUTTERSTOCK ©

Soak up the atmosphere on Venice Boardwalk (p122)

Enjoy the fun of the fair at Santa Monica (p108)

Learn everything about film at the Academy Museum of Motion Pictures (p92)

Go behind the scenes at Universal Studios (p160)

Marvel at the A-list art at Broad (p138)

Admire the art and architecture of the Getty Center (p88)

HAYK_SHALUNTS/SHUTTERSTOCK ©

**Survey
three great
museums at
Exposition
Park (p155)**

**Take in the
wealth of art
at LACMA
(p94)**

ELLIOTT COWAND JR/SHUTTERSTOCK ©

Explore the happiest place on earth at Disneyland® Resort (p170)

ZANE VERGARA/SHUTTERSTOCK ©

SEAN PAVONE/SHUTTERSTOCK ©

Discover the stars at Griffith Observatory (p54)

BENNY MARTY/SHUTTERSTOCK ©

Check out the beauty and beautiful people at Malibu (p168)

Dining Out

LA's table is a global feast. And while there's no shortage of just-like-the-motherland dishes – from xiao long bao to pupusas – it's the takes on tradition that thrill. Ever tried a vegan cream-cheese doughnut with jam, basil and balsamic reduction? LA may be many things, but a culinary bore isn't one of them.

The Big Shots

That LA's food scene is white hot is confirmed by the ever-growing number of top-tier out-of-town chefs opening up in town, among them Michelin-starred San Franciscan Melissa Perello (M.Georgina) and New Yorker David Chang (Majordomo). They're kept in fine company by LA's own homegrown visionaries, from Michelin-starred Michael Cimarusti (Connie & Ted's and Providence) to Nancy Silverton (Osteria Mozza), Mary Sue Milliken and Susan Feniger (Borderhouse Grill and Socalo) and Ori Menashe (Bestia and Bavel).

Food Trucks

Some of the best bites in town come on four wheels, with mobile kitchens serving up a global feast of old- and new-school flavors. Track food trucks at Roaming Hunger (www.roaminghunger. com), or check the websites, Twitter or Instagram feeds of favorites such as Kogi BBQ (www.kogibbq. com), Cousins Maine Lobster (www.cousins mainelobster.com), Mariscos Jalisco (@ MariscosJalisco on Twitter) and Yeastie Boys (www.yeastie boysbagels.com).

Best in Town

Providence Creative, meticulous fare worthy of its two Michelin stars. (p44)

M.Georgina Impeccable produce, smoky accents and flawless cocktails. (p147)

Bestia Cult-status Italian with a side of Downtown warehouse cool. (p148)

Found Oyster Ridiculously fresh seafood in a swinging, wine-bar setting. (p43)

Cassia Smashing East-West fusion in Santa Monica. (p116)

TRAVELPIX/ALAMY ©

Best Old-School Los Angeles

Canter's Open 24/7 with kosher classics, a giant bakery and hipster nightspot, the Kibitz Room. (pictured; p101)

Musso & Frank Grill Direct from Hollywood's Golden Age. (p44)

Bob's Big Boy Googie diner within spitting distance of Warner Bros Studios. (p165)

Original Farmers Market Global flavors at an atmospheric 1930s landmark. (p99)

Best Standout LA Bites

Sonoratown Made-from-scratch Sonora-style tacos and burritos. (p148)

Pine & Crane Taiwanese beef roll. (p59)

Sqirl Burnt brioche with housemade ricotta and jam. (p60)

Howlin' Ray's Phenomenal Nashville-style fried chicken. (p149)

Connie & Ted's Lobster rolls, chowder and oyster Bloody Mary shooters. (p82)

Best Cheap Eats

Joy Fresh, flavor-packed Taiwanese-inspired bites. (p71)

Grand Central Market Bustling undercover hub of global street food. (p147)

Santa Monica Farmers Markets Fresh produce and scrumptious street food just blocks from the beach. (p113)

Parking & Dining

Many restaurants charge up to $10 for valet parking services, and an additional dollar or two tip is customary. To avoid this, try to find street parking, often available nearby.

Bar Open

Whether you're after a craft cocktail made with peanut-butter-washed Campari, or a saison brewed with oolong tea, LA pours on cue. From postindustrial coffee roasters to mid-century lounges, classic Hollywood martini bars and cocktail-pouring bowling alleys, LA serves its drinks with a generous splash of wow.

Specialty Bars

LA claims a growing number of specialty bars, focused on one particular libation. Small-batch coffee is the raison d'être at specialty coffee chains such as Intelligentsia, Verve and Maru, while wine bars like Covell in Los Feliz, Tabula Rasa in Hollywood's Thai Town and Holcomb in Highland Park have become bastions for niche and out-of-the-box vino. Silver Lake claims a dedicated sake bar in Ototo, while the Japanese theme extends to Highland Park's Gold Line, one of a handful of LA bars inspired by Tokyo-style 'listening bars', known for their sharply curated turntable tunes.

Cold-Pressed Juice

Southern California claims to have invented the fruit smoothie, but a much hotter recent trend is cold-pressed juice. While conventional juices are produced using fast-spinning blades to tear apart the produce, cold-pressed juices are made by pressing the liquid. The process reputedly protects the juice from heat and excessive oxidation, resulting in a drink with a greater concentration of vitamins, minerals and live enzymes.

Best Specialty Bars

Varnish Superb cocktails in a secret backroom speakeasy. (p150)

Ototo In-the-know sake and a snug neighborhood vibe. (p62)

El Carmen Solidly stocked tequila and mescal tavern. (p101)

Covell Around 150 wines by the glass. (p62)

RICKY CARIOTI/THE WASHINGTON POST VIA GETTY IMAGES ©

Best for a View

Penthouse Santa Monica Bay from 18 stories up. (p117)

Perch Vintage-inspired glamour atop a Renaissance-Revival high-rise. (p151)

Upstairs at the Ace Hotel Downtown views, powerful cocktails and a safari-inspired fit-out. (p151)

Best Old-School Los Angeles

Musso & Frank Grill A martini-shaking veteran from Hollywood's Golden Age. (p44)

Dresden Legendary mid-century lounge captured in *Swingers*. (p61)

Polo Lounge The Beverly Hills Hotel's legendary bar. (p84)

Tiki-Ti Tiki classics in a tiny, tropical bolthole. (p62)

Best for Beers

Imperial Western Beer Company House brews in a grand old station. (p145)

Venice Ale House Beers on a famous beach. (p131)

Sunset Beer Company Craft brews in a low-key beer shop. (p62)

Best Dive Bars

Frolic Room Anti-glam Hollywood dive frequented by Charles Bukowski. (pictured; p37)

Burgundy Room Hollywood at its old-rocker best. (p48)

Nightlife Tips

o Many bars require proof of age upon entry, no matter how old you look. Always take official photo ID.

o Don't drink and drive. Under California law, the legal blood alcohol limit is 0.08%.

Treasure Hunt

LA is a pro at luring cards out of wallets. After all, how can you not bag that supercute vintage-fabric frock? Or that tongue-in-cheek tote? And what about that mid-century-modern lamp, the one that perfectly illuminates that rare, signed Hollywood film script you scored? Creativity and whimsy drive this town, right down to its inventory.

Keep it Indie, Keep it Local

If you're into shopping with honor, and espouse a 'do no harm' lifestyle, then seek out LA's plethora of independent boutiques. You might find yourself scoring Cali-chic threads and handmade sneakers in Downtown's Arts District; rocker outfits, vintage and jars of artisan jam in Silver Lake and Echo Park; small-batch stationery and outrageous jumpsuits in Highland Park; or fair-trade beach bags in oceanside Venice. Museum shops are also often great for unique, local gifts, from jewelry to ceramics.

Downtown Fashion District

Bargain hunters love the frantic, 100-block warren of fashion in Downtown LA's Fashion District. Deals can be amazing, but first-timers are often bewildered by the district's size. For orientation, check out www.fashiondistrict. org. Sample sales are usually held here on the last Friday of every month from 9am to 3pm, with popular showrooms including the California Market Center, Cooper Design Space, Gerry Building, Lady Liberty Building and New Mart. Upcoming sales are posted on the LA Fashion District Instagram account (www. instagram.com/ lafashiondistrict) and website (www. fashiondistrict.org/ explore/calendar).

Best Coastal Living

Aviator Nation Signature hoodies and casuals. (p132)

Bo Bridges Gallery Coastal art photography. (p135)

JWCOHEN/SHUTTERSTOCK ©

Best Offbeat

Wacko Warehouse of kitsch, with a welcome literary impulse. (p65)

Big Bud Press Retro-inspired jumpsuits, tees and more. (p74)

Best Pre-Loved Finds

Luxe De Ville Impeccably maintained and runway-worthy. (p65)

Lemon Frog Treasure trove of mid-century outfits and accessories. (p65)

It's a Wrap! Cast-offs from real TV shows and movies. (p167)

Amoeba Music Epic repository of vinyl, DVDs, CDs and collectables. (p51)

Best for Local Design

Poketo Curated collections of apparel, homewares and gifts. (p153)

Los Angeles County Store Showcasing the work of LA creatives, from bags to art and edibles. (p64)

Best Bookshops

Last Bookstore in Los Angeles An independent giant in a former bank. (pictured; p153)

Skylight Books Snug, community-minded bookstore with regular events. (p65)

Mystery Pier Books Signed movie scripts and rare first editions. (p87)

Best Shopping Strips

Melrose Ave Celebs, rockers and style mavens. (p102)

Abbot Kinney Blvd Indie boutiques and international flagship stores. (p127)

Row DTLA Niche fashion, design and concept stores in an industrial setting. (p153)

For Kids

Los Angeles is sometimes touted as not especially child friendly, and looking around Rodeo Dr or the Sunset Strip, you might think that young Angelenos have been banished to a gingerbread cottage in the woods. In reality, LA offers a bounty of attractions for young travelers, from theme parks to interactive museums.

Best Districts for Kids

When it comes to engaging younger visitors, not all corners of LA were created equal. Top choices include Santa Monica, home to golden beaches, a much-loved bicycle trail, amusement rides on its eponymous pier and the Cayton Children's Museum (www.caytonmuseum.org). More coastal fun awaits in neighboring Venice, its own assets including fantastic street art and a celebrated skatepark.

Further inland, Hollywood dazzles with its movie-industry landmarks, while Griffith Park offers everything from horseback-riding and hiking to zoo creatures, vintage trains and one of the world's finest planetariums. In Mid-City, the blocks of Wilshire Blvd directly east of Fairfax Ave are known as Museum Row due to the concentration of blockbuster cultural attractions, all within walking distance of each other.

North of Hollywood, the San Fernando Valley offers top-tier theme parks and movie-studio tours. South of LA, Orange County lures with the most magical kingdom of all, Disneyland.

Best Outdoor Fun

Universal Studios Hollywood Movie-themed thrills for young and old. (p160)

Disneyland® Resort World's most fabled theme park. (p170)

Griffith Park LA's attraction-packed communal backyard. (p58)

Santa Monica Pier Amusement rides and a fabulous beach. (pictured; p108)

Echo Park Lake Swan-shaped pedal boats and LA skyline views. (p67)

LUCAS FRANCISCO/SHUTTERSTOCK ©

Warner Bros Studio Tour
Behind-the-scenes look at a working movie studio. (p164)

Best Rainy-Day Adventures

California Science Center
Space shuttle, simulated earthquake and mind-expanding thrills. (p155)

Natural History Museum
Millions of years explored through hands-on exhibits. (p155)

Griffith Observatory Grab a seat in the planetarium by day, peer into telescopes on the lawn at night. (p54)

Museum of Tolerance
Ponder the life and courage of Anne Frank. (p80)

Petersen Automotive Museum Complete with kids' section inspired by the movie *Cars*. (p98)

La Brea Tar Pits & Museum
Child-friendly exhibits for future paleontologists. (p98)

Best for Budding Creatives

Getty Center Hands-on creative fun, a kids' gift shop and play-friendly gardens. (p88)

Broad Pop paintings, giant installations and the fantastical *Infinity Mirrors* room. (p138)

Academy Museum of Motion Pictures Immersive journey through the world of movie making. (p92)

Best Kid-Friendly Eateries

Original Farmers Market
Guaranteed to please the most finicky eaters. (p99)

Grand Central Market
Colorful wonderland of affordable casual bites. (p147)

Eataly LA Everything from pizza and pasta to cannoli under the one *delizioso* roof. (p83)

Bob's Big Boy Fun, classic diner with spot-hitting burgers. (p165)

Canter's Atmospheric Jewish deli with snug booths and a huge menu. (p101)

Salt & Straw Creatively flavored artisan ice cream that's the bomb. (p128)

Active Los Angeles

Despite spending a lot of time jammed on freeways, Angelenos love to get physical. Theirs is a city made for pace-quickening thrills, with spectacular mountain hikes and one of the country's largest urban nature reserves. Add to this almost 300 days of sunshine and you'll forgive the locals for looking so, so good.

Hiking

If hiking doesn't feel like an indigenous LA activity to you, you need to reassess. This town is hemmed in and defined by two mountain ranges and countless canyons, serving up dramatic topography. Most remarkable is the sheer proximity of the city's hiking trails, with rugged, mountain-cat country a mere 2.5 miles north of Hollywood's Capitol Records Building. Add to this near-perfect weather year-round and there are few excuses not to tie those hiking boots.

In the San Gabriel Mountains, trails wind from Mt Wilson into granite peak wilderness, once the domain of the Gabrielino people and the setting for California's last grizzly bear sighting. Its 655,000 acres of wilderness include the Santa Anita Canyon – arguably Southern California's most spectacular river canyon.

The Chumash roamed the Santa Monica Mountains, which are smaller, but still offer spectacular views of chaparral-draped peaks with stark drops into the Pacific. The 67-mile Backbone Trail spans the range, which is known for its spectacular springtime wildflowers.

In Los Angeles itself, Griffith Park (pictured) was gifted to the city in 1896 by mining mogul Griffith J Griffith. It's one of the country's largest municipal parks, with over 50 miles of walking trails, both leisurely and strenuous.

For online advice about hiking trails, check out excellent

Modern Hiker (www.modernhiker.com) and Trails (www.trails.com), and download the AllTrails app.

Skateboarding

Extreme sports in SoCal go back to the 1970s when skateboarders on the Santa Monica–Venice border honed their craft by breaking into dry swimming pools in the backyards of mansions (the 2005 film *Lords of Dogtown* chronicles their rise). Venice remains a hotspot for skaters, its famous 17,000-sq-ft skatepark popular with board masters and their fans. Those wanting to skate its pools and snake run can rent skateboards at Jay's Rentals (http://jaysrentalsvb.com), located steps away on the Venice Boardwalk.

Best City Hikes

Wisdom Tree, Cahuenga Peak & Mt Lee Summit Loop Spectacular and challenging, with dizzying views of the city and mountains and a close-up view of the Hollywood sign. (p41)

Runyon Canyon Short and relatively easy, with good celeb-spotting potential and city views. (p41)

Bronson Canyon An easy option leading to famous caves featured in retro TV hits *Batman* and *The Lone Ranger*. (p59)

Best on Wheels

Venice Skatepark Getting gnarly at LA's world-famous skateboarding mecca. (p123)

South Bay Bicycle Trail Catching a Pacific breeze on this celebrated 22-mile stretch. (p109)

Bikes & Hikes LA Tackling the 32-mile 'LA in a Day' cycling adventure. (p82)

Live Music

The history of music in LA might as well be the history of American music, at least for the last eight decades. Much of the recording industry is based here, and the sheer abundance of world-class musicians, paired with spectacular and historic venues, make it a minor tragedy to leave town without a concert in the memory files.

HARMONY GERBER/SHUTTERSTOCK ©

Musical Choices

In your Los Angeles dream, you're a DJ – so what kind of music do you play? Beach Boys, West Coast rap, original punk, classic soul, hard bop, heavy metal, opera? Try all of the above. To hear the world's most eclectic playlist, just walk down an LA city street. From the electronic mixologists of Echo Park to the LA Phil or a legendary rock-and-roll band – the choice is yours. Download the Bandsintown app for listings.

Best Outdoor Venues

Hollywood Bowl LA's greatest gift to musicians and their fans. (p49)

Greek Theatre More intimate than the Bowl and almost as perfect. (pictured; p63)

Getty Center Free alt rock, world music and DJ sets during summer's Off the 405 series. (p88)

Santa Monica Pier No-fee Wednesday night tunes in late summer. (p118)

Best Indie Venues

El Rey Emerging and big-name acts in an art deco dance hall. (p102)

Echo & Echoplex Edgy mix of DJ-driven dance parties and new rockers. (p64)

Fonda Theatre Anything from singer-songwriters to synth-pop acts and new-school rappers. (p50)

Best Classical & Jazz Venues

Walt Disney Concert Hall Sublime acoustics and world-class home of the LA Philharmonic. (p144)

Vibrato Grill Bar Designed by Grammy Award–winning jazz legend Herb Alpert. (p85)

Beaches

STOCKPHOTOASTUR/SHUTTERSTOCK ©

With miles and miles of wide, sandy beaches, you'll find it hard to resist getting wet in LA. Beach life and surf culture are part of the free-wheeling SoCal lifestyle, so play hooky any day of the week and go hit the waves like the locals so often do.

Surf's Up! You Down?

Surfing tints every aspect of LA beach life, from clothing to lingo. The most powerful swells arrive in late fall and winter, while May and June are generally the flattest months, although they do bring warmer water. Speaking of temperature, without a wet suit, you'll likely freeze your butt off except at the height of summer. Outfitters in Santa Monica, Venice and elsewhere can provide gear and lessons.

Beach Volleyball

Beach volleyball originated in Santa Monica during the 1920s. You'll find nets up and down LA County's beaches, especially in Santa Monica (pictured), Venice and Manhattan Beach, where AVP (Association of Volleyball Professionals; www.avp.com) Pro Beach Volleyball tournaments happen every summer. The courts are open to the public; see https://beaches.lacounty.gov for guidelines.

Best Beaches

Venice Boardwalk Sand, waves, street art and some of Los Angeles' best people-watching. (p122)

Santa Monica State Beach Best choice for families, with the famous pier and its rides close by. (p109)

Manhattan Beach Lots of space, lots of waves and a trendy, salubrious air. (p135)

El Matador Beachcomb on Malibu's most photogenic strip. (p169)

South Venice Beach Bodysurfing waves aplenty, quieter stretches of sand and the near-constant likelihood of a volleyball game. (p125)

Celebrity-Spotting

ALEX MILLAUER/SHUTTERSTOCK ©

Admit it. You want to see a celeb. You're in Hollywood, so don't apologize for it. Maybe it's the talent we love, or feeling connected to the world through one anointed person, or thinking we'll absorb a bit of the holy glow. Or maybe they're just cool, or...hot. So darn hot.

Getting Your Star Fix

So where to look for stars? Restaurants are primo, especially in West Hollywood, Hollywood, Malibu, Los Feliz and Mid-City. Shopping works too, so browse their faves on Robertson Blvd and Abbot Kinney Blvd. The West Hollywood and Pacific Palisades branches of supermarket chain Gelson's (www.gelsons.com) are known for famous shoppers. Finally, hillside trails are favored for working up a sweat.

Popular Celeb-Spotting Spots

Fred Segal Top-shelf shopping yields top-shelf shoppers. (p87)

Runyon Canyon Don't let those shades fool you. Even the stars love hiking. (pictured; p41)

Melrose Ave Paparazzi, skinny jeans, heels and scented candles. (p102)

Nobu Malibu A handy go-to for oceanside stars, with chef Nobu Matushisa's signature treats to boot. (p169)

Oaks Gourmet Hip Hollywood deli popular with famous locals. (p45)

Grove Everyone from Justin Bieber to Kylie Jenner shops at this outdoor mall. (p103)

Television Tapings

○ You're pretty much guaranteed to see a star or two at a live TV-show taping. Apply for tickets well in advance online.

○ If you do get tickets, get there early to land a good seat.

Under the Radar

From smoky market stalls peddling Latin bites to neighborly streets awash with indie-spirited coffee shops, bars and vintage stores, LA is richer than its celeb-centric image.

JIM_BROWN_PHOTOGRAPHY/SHUTTERSTOCK ©

Guatemalan Night Market

Once a glamorous enclave for silent-film stars, Westlake is now Downtown's raffish western neighbor, tempered by MacArthur Park, the very one that 'melts in the dark' in the eponymous Jimmy Webb song made famous by Donna Summer. Despite the whiff of gentrification, the neighborhood remains a gritty bastion of working-class Hispanic *vida*. One of its best-kept secrets is the **Guatemalan**

Night Market (cnr S Bonnie Brae & W 6th Sts, Westlake; dishes around $5; ⏰5pm-late; 🚻; Ⓜ B/D Lines to Westlake/MacArthur Park), where throngs of *jornaleros* (day laborers) head nightly for cheap, authentic Latin American street food such as *longaniza* sausages, *garnachas* (fried corn tortillas topped with ground meat, tomato sauce and pickled cabbage) and *hilachas,* stewed shredded beef with vegetables and mild dried chiles. Bring cash.

Highland Park

Low-rise neighborhood Highland Park is a walkable hub of gentrified Craftsman homes, blog-worthy coffee shops, restaurants, bars and one-off shops, living side by side with throwback taquerias and grocery stores. Most of the action is on York Blvd and Figueroa St. Worthy pitstops include cult-status Taiwanese eatery Joy (p71) and Japanese-inspired listening bar Gold Line (p74).

LGBTIQ+

While your gaydar will be pinging throughout the county, the rainbow flag flies highest in Boystown, along Santa Monica Blvd in West Hollywood. Earthier scenes are found in Silver Lake and Downtown LA.

JOSEPH SOHM/SHUTTERSTOCK ©

LGBTIQ+ Festivals

The festival season kicks off in mid-May with Long Beach Pride (www. longbeachpride. com) and continues with LA Pride (www. lapride.org) in mid-June, bringing huge crowds to West Hollywood (WeHo) for its exhibits, shows and parade down Santa Monica Blvd. May is also time for RuPaul's DragCon (https:// la.rupaulsdragcon. com), the world's largest drag-culture convention. Jump to Halloween (October 31) and around 500,000 outrageously costumed revelers of all persuasions hit Santa Monica Blvd for ghoulish WeHo fun.

Best Nightspots

Abbey It's been called the best gay bar in the world, and who are we to argue? (p86)

Akbar Fun-loving, Casbah-style spot for queer Eastsiders of all ages. (p62)

Precinct Down-n-dirty, rock-and-roll-style bar pulling everyone from twinks to bears. (p151)

Eagle LA As close as LA gets to a proper gay leather bar. (p63)

Best Performances

Celebration Theatre (www. celebrationtheatre.com) Ranks among the nation's leading companies for LGBTIQ+ plays.

Cavern Club Theater (www. cavernclubtheater.com) Drag shows and other fabulously kooky performances beneath a Silver Lake Mexican restaurant.

Gay Men's Chorus of Los Angeles (www.gmcla.org) This world-class ensemble has been singing it loud since 1979.

Tours

Whatever your pleasure – dark or light, tragic or profane, sweet or savoury – there is an LA tour for you. Take a tour of scandal and blood, gawk at the stars (and their dirt) with actual paparazzi, explore a working studio in Burbank or Hollywood or gaze at world-class architecture downtown.

ARCHITECT: FRANK GEHRY;
IMAGE: THOMAS POMPEANI/SHUTTERSTOCK ©

City Overview

Glitterati Tours (www.glitteratitours.com) Private SUV tours offering local insight into LA's diverse neighborhoods.

Architecture

Los Angeles Conservancy (www.laconservancy.org) Walking tours exploring the city's architectural treasures.

Architecture Tours LA (www.architecturetoursla.com) Neighborhood- and architect-themed bus tours for fans of bold, beautiful and unusual buildings.

Art, Culture & Lore

Esotouric (www.esotouric.com) Offbeat bus and walking tours of LA's sometimes gruesome underbelly.

Dearly Departed (www.dearlydepartedtours.com) Frequently hilarious, occasionally creepy tours of Hollywood's dark side.

Pride Explorer (www.thelavendereffect.org/tours) Self-guided walking tours of LA's LGBTIQ+ history.

TMZ Celebrity Tour Fun, paparazzi-inspired tours with celeb-spotting specialists. (p41)

Cycling & Hiking

Bikes & Hikes LA A 32-mile 'LA in a Day' bike tour to kick your butt. (p82)

Film Studios

Warner Bros Studio Tour Snoop around where movie magic is made. (p164)

Paramount Pictures The only studio still in Hollywood proper. (p40)

Food & Drink

Melting Pot Food Tours (www.meltingpottours.com) Culinary adventures in Mid-City, East LA and Pasadena.

Four Perfect Days

Day 1

JAVEN/SHUTTERSTOCK ©

Walk all over your favorite stars on the **Hollywood Walk of Fame** (pictured; p36) and size up their handprints outside **Grauman's Chinese Theatre** (p37). If Hollywood history intrigues, hit the **Hollywood Museum** (p37) and lunch at **Musso & Frank Grill** (p44).

Up your chances of actually spotting celebs on boutique-lined **Melrose Ave** (p102). If your idols are more Kubrick than Kardashian, snub the shops for the extraordinary **Academy Museum of Motion Pictures** (p92).

After dinner at convivial **Connie & Ted's** (p82), split your sides with live comedy at the **Laugh Factory** (p85) or **Improv** (p85).

Day 2

ARCHITECT: FRANK GEHRY. IMAGE: MATTEO.IT/SHUTTERSTOCK ©

Time to hit booming Downtown LA, reserving tickets in advance to the spectacular **Broad** (p138). If modern art doesn't appeal, explore the city's Hispanic roots at **El Pueblo de Los Angeles** (p145).

Following lunch at **Grand Central Market** (p147), take in Broadway's heritage architecture before hitting high notes at the **Grammy Museum** (p145). Alternatively, shop hip stores in the Arts District and the adjacent **Row DTLA** (p153) complex, the latter home to hotspot restaurant **M.Georgina** (p147). Follow with cocktails at sneaky **In Sheep's Clothing** (p151), the LA Phil at **Walt Disney Concert Hall** (pictured; p144) or a basketball game at the **Staples Center** (p152).

Day 3

DOGORA SUN/SHUTTERSTOCK ©

Spend the morning at the **Getty Center** (p88), a spectacular synergy of art, architecture, landscaping and panoramic views. If possible, save your appetite for innovative, produce-driven **Gjusta** (p129) in ever-eclectic Venice.

Satiated, hunt down unique fashion, accessories and art along **Abbot Kinney Blvd** (p127) or stroll, pedal or Rollerblade along the **Venice Boardwalk** (p122), taking in its street art.

Wrap up the day in neighboring Santa Monica, catching another perfect SoCal sunset from **Santa Monica Pier** (pictured; p108) before dinner at **Cassia** (p116) and a memorable toast at rooftop bar **Onyx** (p118).

Day 4

SCULPTOR ARCHIBALD GARNER; IMAGE: S F/SHUTTERSTOCK ©

Roll things out with a **Warner Bros Studio Tour** (p164), snooping around back-lot sets and technical departments and eyeing up some of Hollywood's most famous movie props. If you prefer your studio tours with theme-park rides, opt for nearby **Universal Studios Hollywood** (p160).

If you still have energy, head up to the landmark **Griffith Observatory** (pictured; p54) in time to watch the sun sink over the city before dinner with the locals at cozy **Mess Hall** (p60). Fed, wrap up your adventure with a cocktail and live comedy or music at vintage-inspire **Virgil** (p61).

Need to Know

For detailed information, see Survival Guide (p177)

Language
English

Currency
US dollar ($)

Money
ATMs are widely available and card payment is accepted at most attractions and businesses. Travelers checks (US dollars) and non-local checks are rarely accepted.

Cell Phones
Foreign GSM multiband phones work in the USA. US prepaid rechargeable SIM cards are usually cheaper than using your own network; buy them at major telco or electronics stores.

Time
Pacific Standard Time (GMT/UTC minus eight hours).

Tipping
Tipping is *not* optional. Only withhold tips in cases of outrageously bad service.

Daily Budget

Budget: less than $150
Dorm bed: $35–70
Takeout meal: $6–15
Metro day pass: $7
Some concerts and events: free

Midrange: $150–300
Hotel double room: $200
Two-course dinner and glass of wine: $40
Live music concert: $50

Top end: more than $300
Three-star beach or Downtown hotel: from $300
Dinner at a destination restaurant: from $75, plus drinks

Advance Planning

Three months before Book accommodation and rental car, especially if visiting during busy festival or holiday periods.

One month before Reserve tickets to major performing arts and sporting events. Register for tickets to a live TV-show taping.

Two weeks before Reserve tickets to the Broad art museum, the Frederick R Weisman Art Foundation and any LA Conservancy walking tours. Reserve tables at top restaurants, particularly if dining later in the week.

Arriving in Los Angeles

Most travelers will arrive in Los Angeles via air.

✈ From Los Angeles International Airport (LAX)

Around 30 to 60 minutes south-west of Downtown LA, subject to traffic.

Bus LAX FlyAway runs nonstop to Downtown (Union Station), Hollywood, Van Nuys and Long Beach; times vary, Downtown route 24 hours, Hollywood route 6:15am to 10:15pm; $8 to $9.75. Catch Big Blue Bus Line 3 or Rapid 3 to Venice and Santa Monica; 5am to midnight; $1.25.

Taxi Available 24 hours; around $60 to Downtown LA and Hollywood, around $35 to Venice and around $40 to Santa Monica (excluding tip).

Getting Around

Cars still rule, but LA's public transit options are improving.

🚇 Metro

Metro subway and light rail lines run from 4am or 5am to around 1am. Extended services Friday and Saturday nights. Fares from $1.75.

🚌 Bus

Metro buses run from 4am to 12:30am; some routes terminate earlier, some run all night. Fares from $1.75. Big Blue Buses operate from 5am or 6am to between 6pm and midnight. Fares from $1.25. DASH buses run from 6am or 7am (9am on weekends) to 5pm or 6:30pm. Fare $0.50.

🚕 Taxi

Taxis are expensive. On-demand car-service apps Uber and Lyft are cheaper.

Los Angeles Neighborhoods

Burbank & Universal City (p159)
Home to a theme park, Sushi Row and most of LA's major movie studios. It's also the birthplace of car culture and porn.

West Hollywood & Beverly Hills (p77)
Big dollars and gay fabulous, wonderful shopping, sinful eateries and terrific nightlife, too. From here you can explore the entire city.

Universal Studios

Hollywood Boulevard & the Hollywood Walk of Fame

Getty Center

Academy Museum of Motion Pictures

Los Angeles County Museum of Art (LACMA)

Santa Monica (p107)
Mix with the surf rats, skate punks, yoga freaks, psychics and street performers along a stretch of sublime coastline.

Santa Monica Pier & Beach

Venice Boardwalk

Venice (p121)
Inhale an incense-scented whiff of Venice, a boho beach town and longtime haven for artists, New Agers and free spirits.

Hollywood (p35)

The nexus of the global entertainment industry offers starry sidewalks, blingy nightclubs and celebrity sightings.

Griffith Park, Silver Lake & Los Feliz (p53)

Where hipsters and yuppies collide in an immense urban playground crowned with a window onto the universe.

Griffith Observatory

Highland Park (p69)

Booming northeast neighborhood with some of LA's coolest creative galleries, chic vintage stores and brand-new bars and eateries.

Broad

Exposition Park

Downtown (p137)

Historical, multilayered and fascinating, it's become so cool that the likes of *GQ* have called it America's best downtown.

Miracle Mile & Mid-City (p91)

Museum Row is the big draw, but funky Fairfax and the old Farmers Market are worthy destinations.

Explore
Los Angeles

Worth a Trip 🔭

Los Angeles' Walking Tours 🚶

Hollywood Blvd (p36) EDUARD GORICEV/SHUTTERSTOCK ©

Explore
Hollywood

No other corner of LA is steeped in as much mythology as Hollywood. It's here that you'll find the Hollywood Walk of Fame, the Capitol Records Tower and Grauman's Chinese Theatre, where the hand- and footprints of entertainment deities are immortalized in concrete. Look beyond Hollywood Blvd and you'll discover a multifaceted neighborhood of swinging bistros, maverick galleries and villa-graced side streets littered with Old-Hollywood lore.

The Short List

○ **Paramount Pictures (p40)** *Taking a tour of one of the world's most famous film studios.*

○ **Hollywood Museum (p37)** *Eyeing up Hollywood memorabilia in a former make-up studio for the stars.*

○ **Hollywood Bowl (p49)** *Catching an evening concert at LA's most iconic outdoor amphitheater.*

○ **Grauman's Chinese Theatre (p37)** *Comparing hand and shoe sizes with entertainment legends.*

○ **Musso & Frank Grill (p44)** *Sipping martinis at a dapper veteran of Hollywood's Golden Age.*

Getting There & Around

Ⓜ The B Line (Red) connects Hollywood Blvd to Los Feliz, Downtown LA and Universal Studios.

🚌 Metro Lines 2 and 302 connect Sunset Blvd to West Hollywood and Westwood. Metro Lines 4 and 704 connect Santa Monica Blvd to West Hollywood and Beverly Hills. All four lines reach Silver Lake, Echo Park and Downtown LA. The DASH Hollywood route runs a circuit around Hollywood.

Neighborhood Map on p38

Paramount Pictures (p40) BEKETOFF/SHUTTERSTOCK ©

Top Experience 📷
Go Star-Spotting on Hollywood's Walk of Fame

Over 2600 performers have been honored with a pink-marble sidewalk star on Hollywood's Walk of Fame, its most famous stretch being Hollywood Blvd. Many of the neighborhood's main attractions are clustered near the intersection of Hollywood Blvd and Highland Ave, among them some genuine relics from Hollywood's Golden Age.

◎ MAP P38, B3

www.walkoffame.com

Hollywood Blvd

Ⓜ B Line to Hollywood/Highland

Grauman's Chinese Theatre

Ever wondered what it's like to be in George Clooney's shoes? Just find his footprints in the forecourt of this world-famous **movie palace** (pictured; TCL Chinese Theatre; ☎ 323-461-3331, guided tours 323-463-9576; www.tclchinesetheatres. com; 6925 Hollywood Blvd; admission free; 🚹). The exotic pagoda theater – complete with temple bells and stone heaven dogs from China – has shown movies since 1927 when Cecil B De-Mille's *The King of Kings* first flickered across the screen.

Hollywood Museum

For a taste of Old Hollywood, do not miss this musty **temple to the stars** (☎ 323-464-7776; www.thehollywoodmuseum.com; 1660 N Highland Ave; adult/senior & student/child $15/12/5; ⊙ 10am-5pm Wed-Sun; 🚹), its four floors crammed with movie and TV costumes and props. The museum is housed inside the Max Factor Building, built in 1914 and relaunched as a glamorous beauty salon in 1935. At the helm was Polish-Jewish businessman Max Factor, Hollywood's leading authority on cosmetics. And it was right here that he worked his magic on Hollywood's most famous screen queens.

Dolby Theatre

The Academy Awards are handed out at the **Dolby Theatre** (☎ 323-308-6300; www. dolbytheatre.com; 6801 Hollywood Blvd; tours adult/child $25/19; ⊙ 10:30am-4pm; 🅿), which has also hosted the *American Idol* finale, the ESPY Awards and the Daytime Emmy Awards. The venue is home to the annual PaleyFest, the country's premier TV festival, held in March. Guided tours of the theater will have you sniffing around the auditorium, admiring a VIP room and nosing up to an Oscar statuette.

★ Top Tips

o New Walk of Fame stars are unveiled every two to three months with the help of the celebrities themselves. See the website for updates.

o Download free app Pride Explorer (www. thelavendereffect. org/tours) for an entertaining self-guided walking tour of Hollywood Blvd and surrounds.

✕ Take a Break

Regulars at dive bar **Frolic Room** (☎ 323-462-5890; 6245 Hollywood Blvd; ⊙ 11am-2am; 🛜) have included Frank Sinatra and John Belushi. Select a tune on the jukebox and get friendly with the barkeeps over supercheap drinks.

For a satisfying bite on the go, hit Joe's Pizza (p45) for authentic, New York–style pie, served up whole or by the slice.

For reviews see

◉	Top Experiences	p36
⊙	Sights	p40
✖	Eating	p43
🍷	Drinking	p46
★	Entertainment	p49
🛍	Shopping	p50

Cahuenga Blvd

Hollywood Blvd

28

Hollywood Bowl Rd

N Cahuenga Blvd

Hollywood Fwy

Vine St

Argyle Ave

Whitley Heights

5

Camrose Dr

WHITLEY HEIGHTS

Grace Ave

Hollywood Fwy

Hillcrest Rd

Scenic Gardens Ave

Sycamore

Runyon Canyon

Franklin Ave

Franklin Ave

Whitley Ave

Yucca St

Capitol Records Tower

8

Discover Los Angeles Visitor Information Center

Japan House

7   6   Hollywood/ Highland

12

24

20

Hollywood/ Vine

M

32

Madame Tussaud's

Hollywood Walk of Fame

33   3

TMZ Celebrity Tour

4

Egyptian Theatre

9

Hollywood Blvd

16

30

26

Selma Ave

19

Cosmo St

Vine St

Red Line Tours

35

15

38

W Sunset Blvd

31

HOLLYWOOD

N Fuller Ave

N Poinsettia Pl

N Alta Vista Blvd

N Formosa Ave

N Detroit St

N La Brea Ave

N Orange Dr

N Mansfield Ave

N Highland Ave

14

De Longpre Ave

Delongpre Park

Homeland Ave

Ivar Ave

N Cahuenga Blvd

23

Fountain Ave

Kohn Gallery

Lexington Ave

Hollywood Recreation Center

N Poinsettia Pl

Santa Monica Blvd

The Lot Studios

Regen Projects

37

Romaine St

Eleanor Ave

N Orange Dr

N Mansfield Ave

N Highland Ave

N Sycamore Ave

N Hudson Ave

Wilcox Ave

Cole Ave

Vine St

Willoughby Ave

11

13

Melrose Ave

E
F
G
H

N 0 _____ 500 m
0 _____ 0.25 miles

Griffith
Park

**HOLLYWOOD
HILLS**

N Beachwood Dr

N Gower St

N Bronson Ave

Los Feliz Blvd

Franklin Ave

29 ⬡ ⊗17

Franklin Ave

Franklin Ave

Russell Ave

Yucca St

Hollywood Fwy

Canyon Dr

N Van Ness Ave

Taft Ave

N Wilton Pl

Garfield Pl

N Western Ave

Carlos Ave

21 ⊖

22 ⊖ 3

N Kingsley Dr

Hollywood Blvd

Ⓜ
Hollywood/
Western

🔒 ⬡
36 34
⊖27

Carlton Way

N St Andrews Pl

N Serrano Ave

N Hobart Blvd

N Kingsley Dr

W Sunset Blvd

Afton Pl

N Bronson Ave

N Van Ness Ave

4

Fountain Ave

10 ⊗ ▶
18 ⊗ ▶

N Gower St

N Beachworth Dr

Gordon St

Tamarind Ave

La Mirada Ave

N St Andrews Pl

Lexington Ave

25 ⊖

Virginia Ave

Virginia Ave

5

Santa Monica Blvd

Beth Olam
Memorial
Park

2 ◉
Hollywood
Forever
Cemetery

N Ridgewood Pl

N Western Ave

N Oxford Ave

Lemon Grove
Recreation
Center

Paramount
Pictures
1 ◉

6

E
F
Melrose Ave
G
H

Sights

Paramount Pictures

FILM LOCATION

1 ⊙ MAP P38, E6

Star Trek, Indiana Jones and the *Ironman* series are among the blockbusters that originated at Paramount, the country's second-oldest movie studio and the only one still in Hollywood proper. Two-hour golf-cart tours of the studio complex are offered year-round, taking in the back lots and sound stages. Weekday-only VIP tours (4½ hours) go more in depth and include lunch or hors d'oeuvres. Passionate, knowledgeable guides offer fascinating insights into the studio's history and the movie-making process in general. (☑323-956-1777; www.paramountstudiotour. com; 5555 Melrose Ave; regular/VIP tours $60/189, After Dark tours $99; ⊙tours 9am-3:30pm; 🚌DASH Hollywood/Wilshire Route)

Hollywood Forever Cemetery

CEMETERY

2 ⊙ MAP P38, F5

Paradisiacal landscaping, vainglorious tombstones and epic mausoleums make for an appropriate resting place for some of Hollywood's most iconic dearly departed. Residents include Cecil B DeMille, Mickey Rooney, Jayne Mansfield, punk rockers Johnny and Dee Dee Ramone, and *Golden Girls* star Estelle Getty. Rudolph Valentino lies in the Cathedral Mausoleum (open 10am to 2pm),

Hollywood Forever Cemetery

KC_CLICK/SHUTTERSTOCK ©

while Judy Garland rests in the Abbey of the Psalms. (☎323-894-9507; www.hollywoodforever.com; 6000 Santa Monica Blvd; admission free; ⏰8:30am-5pm Mon-Fri, to 4:30pm Sat & Sun, guided tours 10am most Sat; 🅿🚹; 🚇Metro Line 4, DASH Hollywood/Wilshire Route)

TMZ Celebrity Tour
BUS

3 ◉ MAP P38, B3

Cut the shame; we know you want to spot celebrities, glimpse their homes and laugh at their dirt. Superfun tours by open-sided bus run for two hours, and you'll likely meet some of the TMZ stars...and perhaps even celebrity guests on the bus. Tours depart from beside the El Capitan Theatre, directly opposite the Dolby Theatre. Check the website for additional hours. (☎844-869-8687; www.tmz.com/tour; 6822 Hollywood Blvd; adult/child $52/31; ⏰tours depart 10am-5pm most days; 🚹; Ⓜ B Line to Hollywood/Highland)

Red Line Tours
WALKING

4 ◉ MAP P38, C3

Learn the secrets of Hollywood on Red Line's 'edutaining' Hollywood Behind-the-Scenes Tour, a 75-minute walking tour that comes with nifty headsets to cut out traffic noise. Guides use a mix of anecdotes, fun facts, trivia and historical and architectural data to keep their charges entertained. Its Hollywood Movie Experience – a 90-minute walking tour of Downtown LA – is also outstanding.

Hollywood Hikes

Increase your daily steps with a hike or jog through **Runyon Canyon** (Map p38, A2; www.runyoncanyonhike.com; 2000 N Fuller Ave; ⏰dawn-dusk). Its trails are highly popular with calorie-counting locals, among them Hollywood celebrities. (And you were wondering why one of the three main trails is called the Star Trail.) For a more challenging hike, tackle the spectacular **Wisdom Tree, Cahuenga Peak & Mt Lee Summit** (Wonder View Dr; ⏰dawn-dusk), a rocky, three-mile, hilltop loop that leads to the back of the Hollywood Sign.

(☎323-402-1074; www.redlinetours.com; 6708 Hollywood Blvd; adult/student & senior/child from $27/18/15; ⏰Hollywood Behind-the-Scenes & Hollywood Movie Experience Tours 10am, noon, 2pm & 4pm; 🚹; Ⓜ B Line to Hollywood/Highland)

Whitley Heights
AREA

5 ◉ MAP P38, C2

For a taste of Old Hollywood, wander the narrow, winding streets of Whitley Heights, a residential preservation zone bordered by Franklin Ave to the south, Highland Ave to the west, and split in two by the 101 freeway to the north and east. Peppered with beautiful Moorish, Renaissance and Italianate-style

Gallery Hopping

It's not all 'Lights, camera, action!' in Hollywood, its list of assets also includes prolific commercial galleries specializing in modern and contemporary art. **Regen Projects** (Map p38, B5; ☏ 310-276-5424; www.regenprojects.com; 6750 Santa Monica Blvd; admission free; ☺10am-6pm Tue-Sat; ☐ Metro Lines 4, 237, 704) hosts bold, edgy shows across all mediums, from photography, painting and video art to ambitious installations. It's well known for propelling the careers of some of LA's most successful and innovative artists, among them Matthew Barney, Glenn Ligon and Catherine Opie.

A short walk away, **Kohn Gallery** (Map p38, B5; ☏ 323-461-3311; www.kohngallery.com; 1227 N Highland Ave; ☺10am-6pm Tue-Fri, 11am-6pm Sat; ℗; ☐ Metro Line 237) also offers museum-standard exhibitions, with heavyweights such as Dan Flavin and Barbara Kruger and emerging talents such as Sophia Narrett and Octavio Abúndez on its books.

villas, this was the city's first 'Beverly Hills,' a salubrious estate designed by architect AS Barnes in the early 1900s and inspired by Mediterranean villages. (☐DASH Hollywood Route)

Japan House
CULTURAL CENTRE

6 ◉ MAP P38, B3

This Japanese-government-sponsored institution is tucked away in the Hollywood & Highland Center, by the Dolby Theatre. Its level-two gallery hosts changing exhibits of all things Japanese, from architecture to manga. Three floors up, its sleek, non-lending library houses hundreds of titles on Japanese art, architecture, design, food and more. The library's adjoining terrace offers sweeping views of Hollywood and Downtown, while Japan House's culinary

incubator hosts pop-ups featuring emerging chefs; check the website for upcoming events. (☏800-516-0565; www.japanhousela.com; 6801 Hollywood Blvd, 2nd & 5th fl, Hollywood & Highland Center; admission free; ☺10am-8pm Mon-Sat, to 7pm Sun; ℗; Ⓜ B Line to Hollywood/Highland)

Madame Tussaud's
MUSEUM

7 ◉ MAP P38, B3

The better of Hollywood's two wax museums, this is the place to take selfies with motionless movie stars (Salma Hayek, Tom Hanks and Patrick Swayze), old-school icons (Charlie Chaplin, Marilyn Monroe, Clark Gable), movie characters such as Hugh Jackman's Wolverine from *X-Men*, chart-topping pop stars and all-time-great directors. To save money, book online and opt for the 'Late Night Saver' option, which grants entry after 6pm. (📞323-798-1670; www.madame tussauds.com; 6933 Hollywood Blvd; adult/child $31/24; 🕐10am-8pm; ♿; Ⓜ B Line to Hollywood/Highland)

Capitol Records Tower
LANDMARK

8 ◉ MAP P38, D3

You'll have no trouble recognizing this iconic 1956 tower, one of LA's great mid-century buildings. Designed by Welton Becket, it resembles a stack of records topped by a stylus blinking out 'Hollywood' in Morse code. Some of music's biggest stars have recorded hits in the building's basement studios, including Nat King Cole, Frank Sinatra, the Beatles, Katy Perry and Sam Smith. Outside on the sidewalk, Garth Brooks and John Lennon have their stars. (1750 Vine St; admission free; Ⓜ B Line to Hollywood/Vine)

Egyptian Theatre
LANDMARK

9 ◉ MAP P38, C3

The Egyptian, the first of the grand movie palaces on Hollywood Blvd, premiered *Robin Hood* in 1922. The theater's lavish getup – complete with hieroglyphs and sphinx heads – dovetailed nicely with the craze for all things Egyptian sparked by the discoveries of archaeologist Howard Carter. These days it's a shrine to serious cinema thanks to the nonprofit American Cinematheque. (📞323-466-3456; www.americancinemathequecalendar. com; 6712 Hollywood Blvd; Ⓜ B Line to Hollywood/Highland)

Eating

Found Oyster
SEAFOOD $$

10 ✖ MAP P38, H4

Bonhomie and exceptional seafood are always on the menu at this tiny, always-packed clam shack. Squeeze in among foodies and East Hollywood hipsters for straightforward, produce-driven offerings including Littleneck clams, live Maine scallops, New England–style chowder, lobster bisque rolls and a daily-changing selection of East and West Coast oysters. Head in early (by 5pm in the evenings) or midweek to minimize any wait. (📞323-486-7920; www.foundoyster. com; 4880 Fountain Ave; dishes $7-28; 🕐4-10pm Tue-Thu, to 11pm Fri, noon-11pm Sat, to 10pm Sun; 🚌DASH Hollywood Route, Metro Lines 2, 175)

Petit Trois
FRENCH $$$

11 ✖ MAP P38, B6

Good things come in small packages...like tiny, no-reservations Petit Trois! Owned by acclaimed TV chef Ludovic Lefebvre, its two long counters are where food-lovers squeeze in for smashing, honest, Gallic-inspired grub, from a ridiculously light Boursin-stuffed omelette to standout escargot and a showstopping 'Big Mec' double cheeseburger served with foie-gras-infused red-wine Bordelaise. (📞323-468-8916; www.petittrois.com; 718 N Highland Ave; mains $18-39; 🕐noon-10pm Sun-Thu, to 11pm Fri & Sat; 🅿; 🚌Metro Line 10)

Musso & Frank Grill

EUROPEAN $$$

12 ❌ MAP P38, C3

Hollywood history hangs in the thick air at Musso & Frank Grill, Tinseltown's oldest eatery (since 1919). Charlie Chaplin used to knock back vodka gimlets, Raymond Chandler penned scripts in the high-backed booths, and movie deals were made on the old phone at the back. The menu favors bistro classics, from shrimp cocktail and lobster thermidor to steaks and a decent burger. (📞323-467-7788; www.mussoandfrank.com; 6667 Hollywood Blvd; mains $17-55; ⏰11am-11pm Tue-Sat, 4-9pm Sun; 🅿; Ⓜ B Line to Hollywood/Highland)

Providence

AMERICAN $$$

13 ❌ MAP P38, D6

A modern classic, chef Michael Cimarusti's James Beard–winning, two-Michelin-starred darling is known for turning superlative sea-food into revelatory creations that never feel experimental for the sake of it. Whether it's kampachi paired with black truffle, burdock gelée and Meyer lemon or Santa Barbara spot prawns with sweet pea and mint, flavors conspire in unex-pected, memorable ways worth the hefty price tag. (📞323-460-4170; www.providencela.com; 5955 Melrose Ave; tasting menus lunch $130-190, dinner $190-265; ⏰noon-2pm Fri & 6-10pm Mon-Fri, 5:30-10pm Sat, to 9pm Sun; 🅿; 🚌Metro Line 10)

Luv2eat

THAI $

14 ❌ MAP P38, C4

Don't let the odd name put you off: strip-mall Luv2eat is a vir-tual temple for local Thai foodies. Cordon Bleu–trained Chef Fern and Thailand-raised Chef Pla offer generous serves of dishes not normally seen on LA's Thai menus, from a non-negotiable Phuket-style crab curry to tangy moo-ping (grilled pork skewers). They nail the standards, too, among them a phenomenal papaya salad. (📞323-498-5835; www.luv2eatthai. com; 6660 W Sunset Blvd; mains $9-18; ⏰11am-3:30pm & 4:30-11pm; 🅿🚶🚹; 🚌Metro Lines 2, 302, Ⓜ B Line to Hollywood/Highland)

Stout Burgers & Beers

BURGERS $

15 ❌ MAP P38, D3

Woody, pub-inspired Stout flips gourmet burgers and pours great craft brews. The beef is ground in-house, the chicken is free range and the veggie patties are made fresh daily. The Six Weeker burger (brie, fig jam and caramel-ized onions) and the onion rings are standouts, while the hugely popular happy hour (4pm to 6pm weekdays) slashes food prices in half. (📞323-469-3801; www. stoutburgersandbeers.com; 1544 N Cahuenga Blvd; burgers $12-15, salads $8-12; ⏰11:30am-4am; 🅿🛜🚶; Ⓜ B Line to Hollywood/Vine)

Musso & Frank Grill

Joe's Pizza

PIZZA $

16 MAP P38, C3

Red-neon Joe's pumps out *proper* New York–style pizza by the slice. We're talking hand-tossed, pliable, thin bases, topped with mozzarella, pepperoni and any number of other ingredients. Parmesan and chilli shakers are on standby for those who like it cheesy or hot, with a vegan-cheese pizza option for herbivores. Perfect for a quick, cheap bite on Hollywood Blvd. (323-467-9500; www.joespizza.it; 6504 Hollywood Blvd; pizza slices from $3.50; 11am-2am Sun-Wed, to 3am Thu-Sat; ; M B Line to Hollywood/ Vine)

Oaks Gourmet

DELI $

17 MAP P38, F2

An upbeat hipster deli and wine shop with a devoted following, where you can browse Californian wines, specialty bottled cocktails, artisanal cheeses and other gourmet treats while waiting for your crowd-pleasing BLT (house bacon, tomato, avocado, brie and roasted shallot aioli on toasted sourdough). The breakfast burrito is special and the place is known for the odd celebrity sighting. (323-871-8894; www.theoaks gourmet.com; 1915 N Bronson Ave; sandwiches & salads $12-14; 7am-11pm; P ; DASH Hollywood Route, Metro Line 207)

Square One

CAFE $

18 ✕ MAP P38, H4

On an up-and-coming stretch of Fountain Ave is this homely, indie-spirited brunch favorite with laid-back patio. Eggs feature prominently on the produce-driven, all-day-breakfast menu, from braised mustard and collard greens served with baked eggs and grits, to tacos filled with scrambled eggs and jalapeños. If you're feeling sweet, opt for the French toast or pancakes, both served with proper maple syrup. (☏323-661-1109; www.squareonedining.com; 4854 Fountain Ave; mains $10-17; ⏰8:30am-3pm; ♿🚻; 🚌DASH Hollywood Route, Metro Lines 2, 175)

Hollywood Farmers' Market

MARKET $

19 ✕ MAP P38, D3

LA's largest farmers market is also one of its best, its Sunday-morning sprawl offering organic and specialty produce from scores of local farmers, producers and artisans. Some of the city's top chefs shop here, while its shoppers include the occasional celebrity. The market also offers tasty ready-to-eat bites and drinks, from organic coffee and fresh coconut milk to pastries and freshly shucked oysters. (www.seela.org/markets-hollywood; cnr Ivar & Selma Aves; ⏰8am-1pm Sun; ♿; Ⓜ B Line to Hollywood/Vine)

Drinking

Intelligentsia Coffee

COFFEE

20 ☕ MAP P38, D3

Manna for coffee snobs stuck on Hollywood Blvd, work-friendly Intelligentsia brews beautiful, seasonal beans. Knock back an organic, single-origin Peruvian or perhaps a creamy nitro. Specialty teas, Mr Holmes pastries and a fetching fit-out inspired by French flower painter Paul de Longpré (whose home and flower gardens stood on this very corner) crank up the appeal. (☏213-277-9095; www.intelligentsiacoffee.com; 6401 Hollywood Blvd; ⏰6:30am-7pm; 📶♿; Ⓜ B Line to Hollywood/Vine)

Harvard & Stone

BAR

21 🍸 MAP P38, H3

With daily rotating craft whiskey, bourbon and cocktail specials, Harvard & Stone lures hipsters with its solid live bands, DJs and burlesque troops working their saucy magic on Fridays and Saturdays. Think Colorado ski lodge meets steampunk factory, with a blues and rockabilly soul. Note the dress code, which discourages shorts, shiny shirts, baggy clothes, sports gear and flip-flops. (☏747-231-0699; www.harvardandstone.com; 5221 Hollywood Blvd; ⏰8pm-2am; 📶; Ⓜ B Line to Hollywood/Western)

Tabula Rasa WINE BAR

22 MAP P38, H3

Thai Town's Tabula is everything one could want in a neighborhood wine bar: eclectic drops, unpretentious barkeeps, well-picked tunes on the turntable and regular live gigs (including Sunday jazz). Offerings by the glass are short, sharp and engaging, touching on anything from qvevri-aged Georgian reds to funky Italian orange vino. Beers are equally intriguing and the Cuban sandwich a knockout. (☏213-290-6309; www.tabularasabar. com; 5125 Hollywood Blvd; ⏰5pm-1am Mon-Thu, 2pm-2am Fri & Sat, 2pm-1am Sun; 🛜; 🚌180, 181, 217, 780, Ⓜ B Line to Hollywood/Western)

Sassafras Saloon BAR

23 MAP P38, D5

You'll be pining for the bayou at the moody Sassafras Saloon, where life-size facades channel sultry Savannah. For the full effect, head in on Thursday, when well-made Sazeracs and Vieux Carres are sipped to the sound of live blues. Happy hour (5pm to 8pm) includes $9 selected cocktails, with DJ-spun tunes piquing the party mood on Friday and Saturday. (☏323-467-2800; www.sassafrassaloon.com; 1233 N Vine St; ⏰5pm-2am Tue-Sat; 🛜; 🚋Metro Line 210, Ⓜ B Line to Hollywood/Vine)

Dress Up or Dress Down?

Hollywood's bar scene is diverse and delicious, with a large number of venues on or just off Hollywood Blvd. You'll find everything from historic dive and cocktail bars once frequented by Hollywood legends to velvet-rope hot spots, buzzing rooftop hotel bars and even a rum-and-cigar hideaway. Some of the more fashionable spots have dress codes or reservations-only policies, among them La Descarga (p48). Always check ahead.

No Vacancy BAR

24 MAP P38, C3

If you prefer your cocktail sessions with plenty of wow factor, make a reservation online, style up and head to this old shingled Victorian. It's a vintage-Hollywood scene of dark timber panels and elegant banquettes, with bars tended by clever barkeeps while burlesque dancers and porch-playing musicians entertain the droves of party people. (☏323-465-1902; www. novacancyla.com; 1727 N Hudson Ave; ⏰8pm-2am; 🛜; Ⓜ B Line to Hollywood/Vine)

Hollywood Farmers' Market (p46)

La Descarga   LOUNGE

25 🚇 MAP P38, G5

This mixed-age, reservations-only rum and cigar lounge is a revelation. Behind the marble bar sit more than 1060 types of rum from across the globe. The bartenders mix specialty cocktails, but you'd do well to order something aged and sip it neat as you enjoy live salsa and bachata tunes and, Thursday to Saturday, burlesque ballerinas. Book two weeks ahead for Friday and Saturday. (📞323-466-1324; www.ladescargala.com; 1159 N Western Ave; ⏰8pm-2am Tue-Sat; 🚊Metro Lines 175, 207)

Burgundy Room   BAR

26 🚇 MAP P38, D3

Old Hollywood rocks on at the historic Burgundy Room, a grungy former speakeasy with peeling bar stools, two super-snug booths and restrooms smothered in graffiti. You won't find seasonal cocktails here, just a cool older crowd of rockers and regulars, kicking back cheap (for Hollywood) drinks to blaring blues, indie and classic hard rock. (📞323-465-7530; 1621 1/2 N Cahuenga Blvd; ⏰8pm-2am; 🛜; 🅜B Line to Hollywood/Vine)

Good Times at Davey Wayne's   BAR

27 🚇 MAP P38, E3

Enter the faux garage, walk through the refrigerator door and emerge in a dim, rocking ode to 1970s Californication, complete with pine paneling, 'groovy' wallpaper and enough interior-design kitsch to make your sideburns explode. The draft beers are craft and there's a second bar (housed in a camper) and barbecue on the back deck. Attracts mainly 20- to 30-something hipsters. (☏323-962-3804; www.goodtimesatdaveywaynes.com; 1611 N El Centro Ave; ⏰5pm-2am Mon-Fri, 2pm-2am Sat & Sun; ☏; Ⓜ B Line to Hollywood/Vine)

Entertainment

Hollywood Bowl   CONCERT VENUE

28 ⭐ MAP P38, B1

Summers in LA just wouldn't be the same without alfresco melodies under the stars at the Bowl, a huge natural amphitheater in the Hollywood Hills. Its annual season – which usually runs from late May to September – includes symphonies, jazz bands and iconic acts such as Bob Dylan, Diana Ross and Pet Shop Boys. Bring a sweater or blanket as it gets cool at night. (☏323-850-2000; www.hollywoodbowl.com; 2301 N Highland Ave; rehearsals free, performance costs vary; 🚌Metro Line 237)

Upright Citizens Brigade Theatre   COMEDY

29 ⭐ MAP P38, F2

Founded in New York by *Saturday Night Live* alums Amy Poehler and Ian Roberts along with Matt Besser and Matt Walsh, this sketch-comedy group cloned itself in Hollywood in 2005. With numerous nightly shows spanning anything from stand-up comedy to improv and sketch, it's arguably the best comedy hub in town. Valet parking costs $7. (☏323-908-8702; www.franklin.ucbtheatre.com; 5919 Franklin Ave; tickets $5-12; 🚌Metro Line 207)

Hotel Cafe   LIVE MUSIC

30 ⭐ MAP P38, D3

Cheap cocktails and the chance of catching the next big name in music make this intimate, low-key venue a big hit with insiders and celebrities. It's mainly a stepping stone for promising singer-songwriters and balladeers (a fresh-faced Adele wowed the crowd here back in 2008). Get there early and enter from the alley. Doors usually open between 6:30pm and 8:30pm (check the website). (☏323-461-2040; www.hotelcafe.com; 1623 N Cahuenga Blvd; Ⓜ B Line to Hollywood/Vine)

ArcLight Cinemas   CINEMA

31 ⭐ MAP P38, D4

Assigned seats, exceptional celeb-sighting potential and a varied program that covers mainstream and art-house movies make this 14-screen multiplex the best around. If your taste dovetails with its schedule, the awesome 1963 geodesic Cinerama Dome is a must. Bonuses: occasional Q&As with directors, writers and actors. Parking is $3 for four hours.

(☎323-464-1478; www.arclight cinemas.com; 6360 W Sunset Blvd; Ⓜ B Line to Hollywood/Vine)

Pantages Theatre   THEATER

32 ⭐ MAP P38, D3

The splendidly restored Pantages Theatre is an art deco survivor from the Golden Age and a fabulous place to catch a hot-ticket Broadway musical. Recent shows include *Hamilton*, *My Fair Lady* and *The Cher Show*. (☎information 323-468-1770, tickets 800-982-2787; www.broadwayinhollywood.com; 6233 Hollywood Blvd; Ⓜ B Line to Hollywood/Vine)

El Capitan Theatre   CINEMA

33 ⭐ MAP P38, B3

Disney rolls out family-friendly blockbusters at this movie palace, sometimes with costumed characters putting on the Ritz in live pre-show routines. The best seats are on the balcony in the middle of the front row. VIP tickets ($25) allow you to reserve a seat and include popcorn and a beverage. (☎1-800-3476396; www.elcapitantheatre.com; 6838 Hollywood Blvd; 👪; Ⓜ B Line to Hollywood/Highland)

Fonda Theatre   CONCERT VENUE

34 ⭐ MAP P38, E3

Dating back to the Roaring Twenties, the since-restored Henry Fonda Theatre remains one of Hollywood's best venues for live tunes. It's an intimate, (mostly) general-admission space with an open dance floor and balcony seating. Expect progressive acts such as synth-pop outfit Porches, singer-songwriters like Allen Stone and next-gen rappers like Saint Jhn. (☎323-464-6269; www.fondatheatre.com; 6126 Hollywood Blvd; Ⓜ B Line to Hollywood/Vine)

Catalina Bar & Grill   JAZZ

35 ⭐ MAP P38, C4

It might be tucked in a ho-hum office building (enter through the garage), but once you're inside this sultry premier jazz club all is forgiven. Expect a mix of top touring talent and emerging local acts – performers have included Roy Hargrove, Monty Alexander, Barbara Morrison, Kenny Burrell and Marcus Miller. One or two shows nightly, best reserved ahead. (☎323-466-2210; www.catalinajazzclub.com; 6725 W Sunset Blvd; cover $25-55 plus dinner or 2 drinks; Ⓜ B Line to Hollywood/Highland)

Shopping

Amoeba Music   MUSIC

36 🔒 MAP P38, E3

When a record store not only survives but thrives in this techno age, you know it's doing something right. Flip through 500,000 new and used CDs, DVDs, videos and vinyl at this cult-status music hub, which also stocks band-themed T-shirts, music memorabilia, books and comics. Handy listening stations and the store's outstanding *Music We Like* booklet keep you from buying lemons. (☎323-245-6400; www.amoeba.com; 6200 Hollywood Blvd; ⏰10:30am-11pm Mon-Sat, 11am-10pm Sun; Ⓜ B Line to Hollywood/Vine)

Counterpoint
MUSIC, BOOKS

Woodblock stacks are packed high with used fiction, while crude plywood bins are stuffed with vinyl soul, classical and jazz. Politely ask to see the hidden back rooms, home to the real (albeit pricier) gems. On our last visit to Counterpoint (see 30 ⭐ Map p38, F2) we stumbled across signed, first-edition titles by the late, great Truman Capote. (☎323-957-7965; www.counterpointrecordsandbooks.com; 5911 Franklin Ave; ⏰11am-9pm Mon-Wed, to 11pm Thu-Sun; 🚇Metro Line 207)

JF Chen
DESIGN

37 🔒 MAP P38, B5

A go-to for professional curators, celebrities and their interior decorators, JF Chen offers two cluttered floors of museum-quality furniture and decorative arts from greats such as Poul Kjaerholm, Ettore Sottsass and Charles and Ray Eames. There's never a shortage of extraordinary pieces, whether its a mid-century modern table made of cork or a 1972 leather armchair shaped like a giant baseball glove. (☎323-463-4603; www.jfchen.com; 1000 N Highland Ave; ⏰10am-5pm Mon-Fri, noon-5pm Sat; 🚇Metro Lines 4, 237, 704)

Space 15 Twenty
MALL

38 🔒 MAP P38, D4

This alfresco mini-mall harbors streetwear-cum-skateboard store Pharmacy Boardshop as well as unisex concept store Urban Outfitters. The latter stocks an especially fun selection of tees, sweaters and caps, as well as affordable homewares and gifts, often with a playful edge. The venue is also home to a branch of Umani Burger. (www.space1520.com; 1520 N Cahuenga Blvd; ⏰Pharmacy Boardshop 11am-8pm Mon-Fri, 10am-8pm Sat, 11am-5pm Sun, Urban Outfitters 10am-9pm; 🚇Metro Line 2, Ⓜ B Line to Hollywood/Vine)

Explore ◈
Griffith Park, Silver Lake & Los Feliz

Adorned with stencil art and inked skin, Silver Lake is a hipster enclave, home to buzzing eateries and well-curated boutiques. Just west, easy-living Los Feliz harbors screenwriters, low-key celebrities and some legendary bars. North of Los Feliz lie the canyons and trails of Griffith Park, home of the mighty Griffith Observatory.

The Short List

○ **Griffith Observatory (p54)** *Scanning LA and the galaxy from a world-famous landmark.*

○ **Bronson Canyon (p59)** *Escaping the rat race.*

○ **Hotspot Dining (p59)** *Taste-testing the area's dynamic food scene.*

○ **Retail Therapy (p65)** *Picking up unique wares on Sunset Blvd.*

Getting There & Around

🚌 Metro Lines 2, 4, 302 and 704 run along Sunset Blvd; 2 and 302 buses switch to Santa Monica Blvd. Lines 2 and 302 reach Hollywood, West Hollywood and Westwood. Lines 4 and 704 reach Hollywood, West Hollywood and Beverly Hills. All reach Echo Park and Downtown LA.

Ⓜ The B Line (Red) connects to Hollywood, Universal Studios and Downtown LA. Vermont/Santa Monica station lies 0.7 miles west of Sunset Junction in Silver Lake. Alight at Vermont/Sunset station for Los Feliz.

Neighborhood Map on p56

Griffith Observatory (p54) ARCHITECT: JOHN C AUSTIN:

Top Experience 📷

Discover the Stars at Griffith Observatory

LA's landmark 1935 observatory opens a window onto the universe from its perch on the southern slopes of Mt Hollywood. It also offers a prime view of the 50ft-tall, sheet-metal Hollywood Sign, an LA icon that first appeared in the hills in 1923 as an advertising gimmick for a real-estate development called 'Hollywoodland.'

◎ MAP P56, C4

☏ 213-473-0890

www.griffithobservatory.org

2800 E Observatory Rd

admission free, planetarium shows adult/child $7/3

⊙ noon-10pm Tue-Fri, 10am-10pm Sat & Sun

🚌 DASH Observatory/Los Feliz Route

Samuel Oschin Planetarium

The observatory's planetarium is one of the world's finest, with a state-of-the-art Zeiss star projector, digital projection system and high-tech aluminum dome that transforms into a giant screen that feels impressively realistic. Three daily shows are offered: *Centered in the Universe* takes visitors back to the Big Bang, *Water Is Life* will have you searching for H_2O in the solar system, while *Light of the Valkyries* explores the phenomenon of the Northern Lights.

Leonard Nimoy Event Horizon Theater

The observatory's lower levels were added during an ambitious restoration, which included lifting the entire building off its foundations. Insight is offered in a 23-minute documentary screened in the Leonard Nimoy Event Horizon Theater, which also sheds light on the observatory's founder, Griffith J Griffith. What the film doesn't do is dwell on Griffith's problematic life, which included alcoholism, paranoid delusions and the attempted murder of his wife, Mary Agnes Christina Mesmer.

Telescopes, Views & Jimmy Dean

The rooftop viewing platform offers prime-time views of LA and the Hollywood Hills. Visitors are welcome to peer into the Zeiss Telescope on the east side of the roof, while after dark, staff wheel additional telescopes out to the front lawn for stargazing. LA's hulking deco observatory is no stranger to the spotlight itself, having made cameos in numerous movies and TV shows, among them *La La Land*, *Terminator*, *Beverly Hills 90210*, *24* and *Alias*. The film it's most associated with, however, remains *Rebel Without a Cause*, commemorated with a bust of James Dean on the west side of the observatory lawn.

★ **Top Tips**

o Head up on a clear day to make the most of the spectacular views and stargazing.

o If you're driving and only heading up for the views, do so on a weekday before noon (when the observatory opens) for easier parking.

o During opening hours, parking can be a trial, especially on weekends. Consider catching the DASH Observatory/Los Feliz shuttle bus from Vermont/Sunset metro station or hike up from Los Feliz below.

✗ **Take a Break**

While there's a nondescript cafe at the observatory, a better option is to follow the signposted 0.6-mile hike down to Fern Dell Dr for freshly baked goods at outdoor, counter-service cafe **Trails** (📞 323-871-2102; www.facebook.com/TheTrailsCafe; 2333 Fern Dell Dr, Los Feliz; pastries from $4, meals $5-10; ⏰ 8am-5pm; 📶 👪).

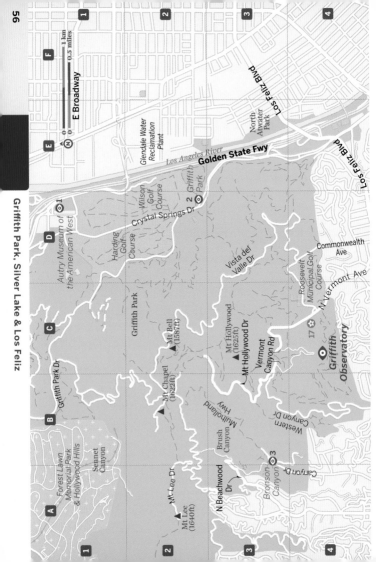

Griffith Park, Silver Lake & Los Feliz

E Broadway

1 km
0.5 miles

Glendale Water
Reclamation Plant

Los Angeles River

Golden State Fwy

North
Atwater Park

Los Feliz Blvd

Los Feliz Blvd

Autry Museum of
the American West

Wilson
Golf Course

Griffith Park

Crystal Springs Dr

Harding Golf
Course

Griffith Park

Vista del
Valle Dr

Commonwealth
Ave

Roosevelt
Municipal Golf
Course

N Vermont Ave

Griffith Park Dr

Mt Bell
(1587ft)

Mt Hollywood Dr

Mt Hollywood
(1625ft)

Vermont
Canyon Rd

Griffith
Observatory

Forest Lawn
Memorial Park
& Hollywood Hills

Sennet
Canyon

Mt Chapel
(1622ft)

Mulholland
Hwy

Western Canyon Dr

Mt Lee Dr

Brush
Canyon

N Beachwood
Dr

Bronson
Canyon

Canyon Dr

Mt Lee
(1640ft)

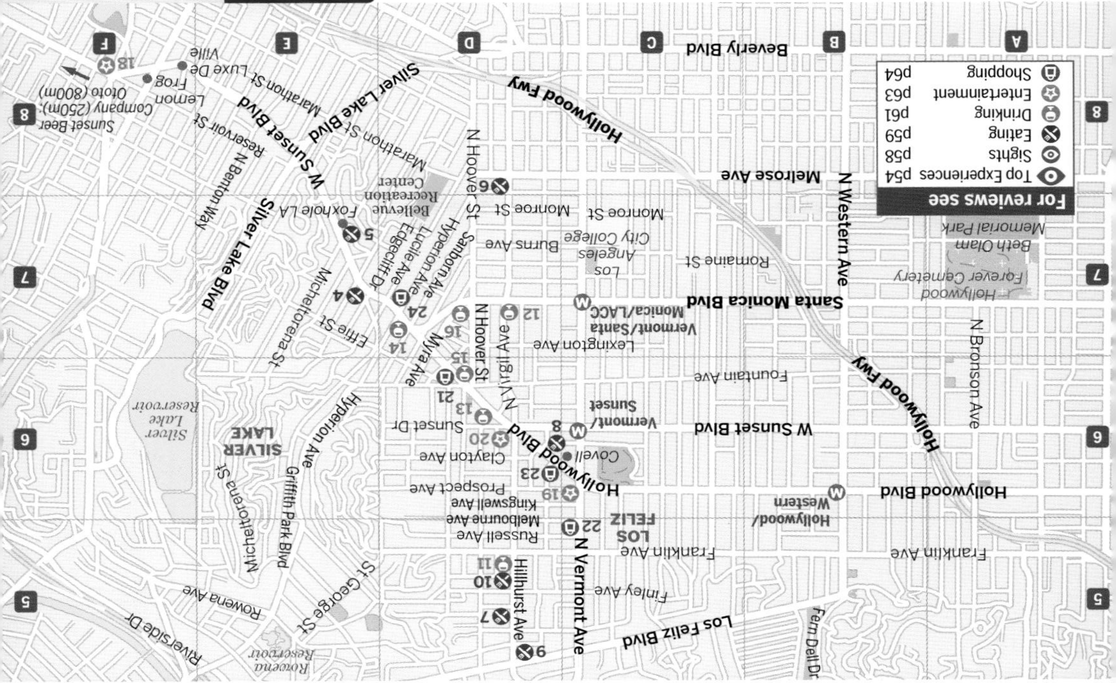

Griffith Park, Silver Lake & Los Feliz

Silver Lake Reservoir

Rowena Reservoir

Riverside Dr

Rowena Ave

St George St

SILVER LAKE

Micheltorena St

Griffith Park Blvd

Hyperion Ave

Micheltorena St

Silver Lake Blvd

Effie St

W Sunset Blvd

Foxhole LA

Reservoir St

N Benton Way

Sunset Beer Company (250m); Ototo (800m)

Lemon Frog

Luxe De Ville

F

18

Bellevue Recreation Center

Marathon St

Marathon St

Edgecliff Dr

Lucile Ave

Hyperion Ave

Sanborn Ave

W Sunset Blvd

Silver Lake Blvd

E

4

5

14

24

Sunset Dr

Clayton Ave

Prospect Ave

Myra Ave

N Hoover St

N Virgil Ave

13

20

21

15

16

6

D

Los Feliz Blvd

Finley Ave

Franklin Ave

Russell Ave

Melbourne Ave

Kingswell Ave

LOS FELIZ

Hollywood Blvd

Covell Ave

Vermont/Sunset

N Vermont Ave

6

7

10

11

Hillhurst Ave

19

22

23

8

Hollywood/Western

Fountain Ave

Lexington Ave

W Sunset Blvd

12

N Virgil Ave

Santa Monica Blvd

Vermont/Santa Monica/LACC

Los Angeles City College

Burns Ave

Monroe St

Monroe St

C

Fern Dell Dr

Franklin Ave

Hollywood Blvd

Hollywood Fwy

N Bronson Ave

Romaine St

Santa Monica Blvd

N Western Ave

Melrose Ave

Beverly Blvd

B

Hollywood Forever Cemetery

Beth Olam Memorial Park

Hollywood Fwy

A

Hollywood Fwy

Los Angeles City College

Hollywood Fwy

N Hoover St

For reviews see

⊙ Top Experiences	p54
⊙ Sights	p58
⊗ Eating	p59
⊙ Drinking	p61
⊙ Entertainment	p63
⊙ Shopping	p64

Sights

Autry Museum of the American West

MUSEUM

1  MAP P56, D1

Established by singing cowboy Gene Autry, this expansive, thoroughly underrated museum offers contemporary perspectives on the history and people of the American West, as well as their links to today's culture. Permanent exhibitions span Native American traditions to 19th-century cattle drives, daily frontier life (look for the beautifully carved vintage saloon bar) to costumes and artifacts from Hollywood westerns. Blockbuster temporary exhibits include the annual Autry Masters Art Exhibition and Sale, showcasing the work of contemporary artists exploring Western themes. (📞323-667-2000; www.theautry.org; 4700 Western Heritage Way, Griffith Park; adult/senior & student/child $14/10/6, 2nd Tue of month free; ⏱10am-4pm Tue-Fri, to 5pm Sat & Sun; 🅿♿; 🚉Metro Line 96)

Griffith Park

PARK

2  MAP P56, D2

Five times the size of New York's Central Park and home to the Griffith Observatory (p54), Greek Theatre (p63) and Autry Museum, LA's communal backyard covers over 4300 acres of land, with over 50 miles of hiking trails. It's where you'll find the **LA Zoo** (📞323-644-4200; www.lazoo.org; 5333 Zoo Dr; adult/senior/child $22/19/17; ⏱10am-5pm; 🅿♿; 🚉Metro Line

Griffith Park

HANNATOR/SHUTTERSTOCK ©

96), quaint train museum **Travel Town** (323-662-5874; www.traveltown.org; 5200 W Zoo Dr; admission free; 10am-4pm Mon-Fri, to 6pm Sat & Sun Mar-Oct, to 5pm Sat & Sun Nov-Feb; P) and the richly festooned, 1926-vintage **Griffith Park Merry-Go-Round** (323-665-3051; www.facebook.com/GriffithParkMGR; 4730 Crystal Springs Dr; rides $2; 11am-5pm daily early Jun-Aug, Sat & Sun Sep-early Jun; P ; Metro Line 96), frequented by Walt Disney and his young daughters and the reputed inspiration for his future Anaheim theme park.

Gifted to the city in 1896 by mining mogul Griffith J Griffith, the park is considered a rare example of unspoilt chaparral. (323-644-2050; www.laparks.org/griffithpark; 4730 Crystal Springs Dr; admission free; 5am-10:30pm, trails sunrise-sunset; P)

Bronson Canyon

HIKING

3 MAP P56, B3

Although most of the pretty people prefer to do their running, walking and hiking in Runyon Canyon, we prefer Bronson. A wide fire road rises to a lookout point and links to the Hollywood sign, Griffith Park and the famed **Bronson Caves** – where scenes from the old *Batman* and *The Lone Ranger* series were shot. (818-243-1145; www.laparks.org; 3200 Canyon Dr; 5am-10:30pm)

Eating

Pine & Crane

TAIWANESE $

4 MAP P56, E7

You'll be licking chopsticks at this hip, unfussy hot spot for Taiwanese-inspired small plates, noodles and rice-based dishes. Feast on spicy shrimp wontons, nutty *dan dan* noodles and the unmissable beef roll, a burrito-like concoction packed with tender beef, cucumber, cilantro, scallions and piquant hoisin sauce. It gets crazy busy, especially at night, so consider heading in for an early lunch. (323-668-1128; www.pineandcrane.com; 1521 Griffith Park Blvd, Silver Lake; dishes $5-14; noon-10pm Wed-Mon; ; Metro Lines 2, 4)

Night + Market Song

THAI $

5 MAP P56, E7

After cultivating a cult following in WeHo, this gleefully garish temple to real-deal Thai and Cambodian street food expanded to the hipster heartlands. Years later, it's still killing it with zingy, palate-pleasing dishes such as spicy larb (minced-meat salad), proper pad Thai and harder-to-find specialties such as Isaan-style fermented pork sausage. To minimize the wait, head in early (before 7pm). (323-665-5899; www.nightmarketla.com; 3322 Sunset Blvd, Silver Lake; dishes $8-16; noon-3pm Mon-Fri & 5-11pm Mon-Sat; ; Metro Lines 2, 4)

Sqirl

CAFE $

6 MAP P56, D8

Despite its somewhat obscure location, this tiny, subway-tiled cafe is forever pumping thanks to its top-notch, out-of-the-box breakfast and lunch offerings. Join the queue to order made-from-scratch wonders such as long-cooked chicken and rice porridge served with dried lime, ginger, turmeric, cardamon ghee and tomato or the cult-status ricotta toast, a symphony of velvety housemade ricotta, thick-cut brioche and Sqirl's artisanal jams. (323-284-8147; www.sqirlla.com; 720 N Virgil Ave; dishes $8-16; 6:30am-4pm Mon-Fri, 8am-4:30pm Sat & Sun; ; B Line to Vermont/Santa Monica)

All Time

CALIFORNIAN $$

7 MAP P56, D5

All Time is always busy. The vibe is casual and continental, and the offerings feel good, fresh and locavore. Breakfast or lunch, tuck into fried-egg breakfast sandwiches, French toast with proper maple syrup or a 'good ass' salad made with just-picked produce from the garden. Dinner is pricier, with a short, market-driven menu that might include superb, housemade cavatelli with slow-cooked lamb ragù. (323-660-3868; www.alltimelosangeles.com; 2040 Hillhurst Ave, Los Feliz; dishes day $10-24, dinner $16-42; 7am-10pm, kitchen closes 8pm; ; Metro Lines 180, 181)

HomeState

TEX-MEX $

8 MAP P56, D6

Texan expat Briana Valdez is behind this rustic ode to the Lone Star State, where locals queue patiently for authentic breakfast tacos such as the Trinity, a handmade flour tortilla topped with organic egg, bacon, potato and cheddar. Then there's the *queso* (melted cheese) and our lunchtime favorite, the brisket sandwich, a coaxing combo of shredded meat, cabbage slaw, guacamole and pickled jalapeños. (323-906-1122; www.myhomestate.com; 4624 Hollywood Blvd, Los Feliz; tacos $3.50, dishes $7-11; 8am-10pm; ; B Line to Vermont/Sunset)

Mess Hall

PUB FOOD $$

9 MAP P56, D5

What was formerly the Brown Derby, a swing dance spot made famous by the film *Swingers*, is now a wonderfully convivial, cabin-style hangout with snug booths, TV sports and a comfy, neighborly vibe. The feel-good factor extends to the menu, with standouts that include comforting mac 'n' cheese and smoky baby-back ribs with slaw and house fries. Head in on Tuesdays for $1 oysters and tacos. (323-660-6377; www.messhallkitchen.com; 4500 Los Feliz Blvd, Los Feliz; mains $17-32; 9am-10pm Sun-Thu, to 11pm Fri & Sat; ; Metro Lines 180, 181)

Jeni's Splendid Ice Creams

ICE CREAM $

10 ❌ MAP P56, D5

There's nothing vanilla about this Ohio import, peddling some of LA's most out-there ice-cream flavors. Live a little with a scoop or three of creamy brown-butter almond brittle, goat's cheese with red cherries or brandied banana brûlée. Then again, the wildberry lavender, gooey butter cake and pineapple upside-down cake all sound good, too. Tough gig. (☏323-928-2668; www.jenis.com; 1954 Hillhurst Ave, Los Feliz; ice cream from $5.75; ⊗noon-10pm Mon-Thu, 11am-11pm Fri-Sun; 🚻; 🚇Metro Lines 180, 181)

Drinking

Maru Coffee

COFFEE

11 ☕ MAP P56, D5

In a mellow, minimalist space of timber and concrete, Maru brews superb specialty coffee, poured into handmade Portland ceramics. Both the espresso and pour-over are some of the best in LA, with other offerings including beautiful teas and matcha lattes. Beans are roasted in small batches at Maru's second, larger location in Downtown's Arts District. (☏323-741-8483; www.marucoffee.com; 1936 Hillhurst Ave, Los Feliz; ⊗7am-6pm Mon-Sat, 8am-6pm Sun; 📶; 🚇Metro Lines 180, 181)

Virgil

BAR

12 🍸 MAP P56, D7

A vintage-inspired hangout with farm-to-bar cocktails and a stocked calendar of top-notch comedy, live music and DJs. Highlights include Monday's Hot Tub variety show, hosted by Kurt Braunohler and Kristen Schaal (the latter of *Flight of the Conchords* fame) and featuring an eclectic lineup of oft-irreverent stand-up comics. Other rotating events include the monthly That's Huge, a free comedy night featuring prolific acts. (☏323-660-4540; www.thevirgil.com; 4519 Santa Monica Blvd, Silver Lake; ⊗7pm-2am; 🚇Metro Line 4)

Tiki-Ti

BAR

13 🍸 MAP P56, D6

Channeling Waikiki since 1961, this tiny tropical tavern packs in everyone from Gen-Y hipsters to grizzled old-timers in 'non-ironic' Hawaiian shirts. Drinks are strong and smooth; order the tequila-fueled Blood and Sand and expect a ritual that involves raucous cheers of 'Toro.' The brown-paper tags are notes written by regulars, some of them dating back to the '60s. Cash only. (☏323-669-9381; www.tiki-ti.com; 4427 W Sunset Blvd; ⊗4pm-2am Wed-Sat; 🚇2, 175, 302, Ⓜ B Line to Vermont/Sunset)

Specialty Drinking Dens

Oenophiles will find their happy place at Los Feliz bar **Covell** (Map p56, C6; ☏323-660-4400; www.barcovell.com; 4628 Hollywood Blvd; ⏰5pm-midnight Sun-Thu, to 2am Fri & Sat; Ⓜ B Line to Vermont/Sunset), its 150-or-so wines by the glass showcasing interesting producers, unusual grapes and lesser-known regions. Just east of Silver Lake in Echo Park, beer-store-cum-bar **Sunset Beer Company** (off Map p56, F8; ☏213-481-2337; www.sunsetbeerco.com; 1498 Sunset Blvd, Echo Park; ⏰4-11pm Mon-Thu, 2pm-midnight Fri, 1pm-midnight Sat, to 10pm Sun; 📶; 🚇Metro Lines 2, 4) offers exceptional craft beers, while snug sake bar **Ototo** (off Map p56, F8; ☏213-784-7930; www.ototo.la; 1360 Allison Ave, Echo Park; ⏰5:30-11pm Mon-Sat, 2-9pm Sun; 📶; 🚇Metro Lines 2, 4, 302, 704) pours a rotating selection of Japanese rice wines. On Sunday afternoons between 2:30pm and 5:30pm, Ototo runs a 'sake school,' with themed sake flights ($18) for the rice-wine curious.

Black Cat

BAR

14 🚇 MAP P56, D7

In 1966, two years before New York's Stonewall Riots, LGBTIQ+ protesters bravely stood up to police harassment at this very site. These days, the Black Cat is an inclusive neighborhood favorite, with a loyal local following, vintage interiors and people-watching seats out front. Great for happy hour (4pm to 6pm), with $6 beers, $8 cocktails and a $9 raclette-laced burger. (☏323-661-6369; www.theblackcatla.com; 3909 W Sunset Blvd, Silver Lake; ⏰4pm-2am Mon-Thu, 2pm-2am Fri-Sun; 📶; 🚇Metro Lines 2, 4, 302, 704)

Akbar

GAY & LESBIAN

15 🚇 MAP P56, D6

Fun-loving, Casbah-style Akbar is a hit with queer Eastsiders of all ages – hipsters, greying daddies, skyscraping drag queens. It's diverse, attitude free and a refreshing antidote to the look-at-me WeHo scene. There's no shortage of themed nights, from lip-sync comps and karaoke to late-week dance sessions with gyrating go-go boys. (☏323-665-6810; www.akbarsilverlake.com; 4356 W Sunset Blvd, Silver Lake; ⏰4pm-2am; 🚇Metro Lines 2, 175, 302)

Eagle LA

GAY

16 🚇 MAP P56, D7

A dark, sexy demimonde where the walls are black, the lights red and the videos hardcore, the Eagle is as close as LA gets to a proper gay leather bar, especially on themed nights (see the website). It's a friendly neighborhood hangout, with pool table, the odd topless-bear barkeep and a crowd of mixed body types and ethnicities. Cash only. (☎323-669-9472; www.eaglela.com; 4219 Santa Monica Blvd, Silver Lake; ⏰4pm-2am Mon-Fri, 2pm-2am Sat & Sun; 📶; 🚇Metro Line 4)

Entertainment

Greek Theatre
LIVE MUSIC

17 ⭐ MAP P56, C4

The 'Greek' in the 2010 film *Get Him to the Greek* is this 5900-capacity outdoor amphitheater, tucked into a woodsy Griffith Park hillside. A more intimate version of the Hollywood Bowl, it's much loved for its vibe and variety – recent acts include Gladys Knight, Alicia Keys, John Legend and Adam Ant. Parking is stacked, so plan on a postshow wait. Alternatively, regular shuttle buses run between the venue and the

cheaper off-site Pony Ride Train parking lot from two hours before show time to 30 minutes after the show. (☎844-524-7335; www.lagreektheatre.com; 2700 N Vermont Ave; ⏰late Apr–mid-Oct; 🚌DASH Observatory/Los Feliz Route)

Echo
LIVE MUSIC

18 ⭐ MAP P56, F8

Eastsiders hungry for an eclectic alchemy of sounds pack this crowded dive, basically a sweaty bar with a stage and a back patio. On the music front, expect anything from indie and electronica to dub reggae and dream and power pop. Monday nights are dedicated to up-and-coming local bands, with regular club nights including Saturday's always-a-blast Funky Sole party. Downstairs lies sister

Akbar

Griffith Park, Silver Lake & Los Feliz Entertainment

venue Echoplex, entered separately from the alley at 1154 Glendale Blvd, just around the corner. (www.spaceland andpresents.com; 1822 W Sunset Blvd, Echo Park; cover varies; 🚇 Metro Lines 2, 4, 302, 704)

Rockwell
LIVE MUSIC

19 ⭐ MAP P56, C6

If you like to be entertained while you chew, make a reservation at this table and stage, serving up a mixed bag of cabaret, Broadway tunes and musical parodies. On selected Wednesday evenings, Hollywood veteran Jeff Goldblum and his Mildred Snitzer Orchestra take to the stage, charming the crowd with smooth jazz and the opportunity for fan selfies; see the website for dates. (📞323-669-1550; www.rockwell-la.com; 1714 N Vermont Ave, Los Feliz; Ⓜ B Line to Vermont/Sunset)

Vista Theatre
CINEMA

20 ⭐ MAP P56, D6

Dating back to 1923, the single-screen Vista has played some colorful roles, nominally vaudeville theater and gay-porn cinema. It's now back to screening mainly mainstream new releases in its wonderfully kitsch 'ancient Egyptian' interior. At the front is a humbler, more indie-oriented version of Hollywood's Chinese Theatre forecourt, with the concrete imprints of names such as Spike Jonze. (📞323-660-6639; www.vintagecinemas.com/vista; 4473 W Sunset Blvd, Los Feliz; 🚇 Metro Lines 2, 175, 302, Ⓜ B Line to Vermont/Sunset)

Shopping

Los Angeles County Store
GIFTS & SOUVENIRS

21 🔒 MAP P56, D6

If you love supporting local makers (and you should!), make time for this strip-mall treasure. On the back wall, a giant map of LA marks the store's current crop of artists and artisans, their well-made wares ranging from leather goods, stationery, art prints and photography to LA-themed tees, cushions, picture books and chocolate blocks. Prices are reasonable and the stock varied and fun. (📞323-928-2781; www.lacountystore.com; 4333 W Sunset Blvd, Silver Lake; ⏱11am-6pm Tue-Sat, to 5pm Sun; 🚇 Metro Lines 2, 175)

Skylight Books
BOOKS

22 🔒 MAP P56, C5

Occupying two adjoining shopfronts, this much-loved Los Feliz institution carries everything from art, architecture and fashion tomes, to LA history titles, vegan cookbooks, queer literature and critical theory. There's a solid selection of niche magazines and local zines, some great lit-themed tees and regular, engaging in-store readings and talks (with the podcasts uploaded onto the store's website). (📞323-660-1175; www.skylightbooks.com; 1818 N Vermont Ave, Los Feliz; ⏱10am-10pm; Ⓜ B Line to Vermont/Sunset)

Wacko

COLLECTIBLES

23 🔒 MAP P56, D6

Billy Shire's sprawling giftorium of pop, kitsch and camp has been a fun browse for decades. Pick up a Ziggy Stardust T-shirt, a *Star Wars* tote or perhaps a latex unicorn mask. You'll find a great selection of comics and books, including works by LA authors such as Ray Bradbury, Philip K Dick and Dan Fante.

Out back is **La Luz de Jesus**, one of LA's top lowbrow-movement art galleries. The gallery's opening parties (on the first Friday of the month) are the stuff of local legend. (📞323-663-0122; www.soap plant.com; 4633 Hollywood Blvd, Los Feliz; ⏰11am-7pm Mon-Wed, to 9pm Thu, to 10pm Fri & Sat, noon-6pm Sun; Ⓜ️B Line to Vermont/Sunset)

Matrushka

FASHION & ACCESSORIES

24 🔒 MAP P56, D7

Writers, film-industry types and independent style queens love Matrushka, a boutique and workshop owned and run by designer Lara Howe. Chances are you'll find her at her sewing machine, creating frocks, jumpsuits, leggings and

Marvellous VintageVille

Silver Lake and neighboring Echo Park claim a string of renowned vintage stores. Standouts include **Luxe de Ville** (Map p56, F8; 📞213-353-0135; 2157 Sunset Blvd, Echo Park; ⏰noon-7pm Mon-Fri, 11am-7pm Sat, to 5pm Sun; 🚇Metro Lines 2, 4, 302, 704), **Lemon Frog** (Map p56, F8; 📞213-413-2143; www.lemonfrogshop.com; 1202 N Alvarado St, Echo Park; ⏰10:30am-5pm Mon-Sat, noon-5pm Sun; 🚇Metro Lines 2, 4, 302, 704) and **Foxhole LA** (Map p56, E7; 📞213-290-7175; www.foxholela.com; 3318 W Sunset Blvd, Silver Lake; ⏰hours vary, generally noon-4pm Mon-Wed, Fri & Sat; 🚇Metro Lines 2, 4).

more, using bold, vintage-inspired fabrics. The pieces are fabulously affordable and Lara can sew pieces to size (taking a few days to a few weeks). (📞323-665-4513; www.matrushka.com; 3822 W Sunset Blvd, Silver Lake; ⏰11am-7pm Mon-Fri, to 6pm Sat & Sun; 🚇Metro Lines 2, 4, 302, 704)

Walking Tour 🥾

Cruising Echo Park

If you dig the uneasy interface of urban art, music and hipster culture in multiethnic neighborhoods, you'll love Echo Park, punctuated by the fountain lake featured in Polanski's Chinatown. True, the artists and cool hunters have settled in, but the panaderías and cevicherías happily remain.

Walk Facts

Start Eightfold Coffee;
🚊 Metro Lines 2, 4, 302, 704

Finish Luxe De Ville;
🚊 Metro Lines 2, 4, 302, 704

Length 1.8 miles;
four hours

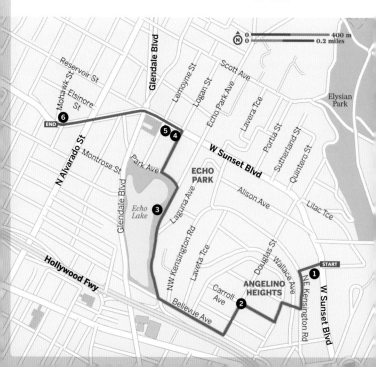

❶ Joe & Jewels

Eastside stylists and musicians flock to minimalist, whitewashed **Eightfold Coffee** (☏213-947-3500; www.facebook.com/eightfoldcoffee; 1294 Sunset Blvd, Echo Park; ☺7am-6pm Mon-Sat, to 5pm Sun; 🛜) to talk gigs and sip superlative joe. Order one to go and check out the imaginative artisan jewelry at neighboring **Esqueleto** (☏213-947-3508; www.shopesqueleto.com; 1298 Sunset Blvd, Echo Park; ☺11am-7pm Mon-Thu, to 6pm Fri-Sun).

❷ Painted Ladies

Stairs beside Esqueleto lead up to Angelino Heights, established in the mid-1880s as one of LA's first suburbs. Its most charming street is **Carroll Ave**, home to the largest concentration of Victorian-era homes in the city. Number 1345 appears in Michael Jackson's *Thriller* music video, while number 1329 moonlights as Halliwell Manor in TV series *Charmed*.

❸ Echo Park Lake

A former reservoir, **Echo Park Lake** (www.laparks.org; 751 Echo Park Ave, Echo Park; 🅿🚻) is best known as the setting for Jake Gittes' surreptitious rowboating shenanigans in Polanski's classic film *Chinatown,* and for its keyhole vistas of the Downtown skyline. Find the boathouse and rent a swan-shaped pedal boat.

❹ Local Fare & Brews

If you're hungry, slip into loft-like **Sage** (☏213-989-1718; www.sageveganbistro.com; 1700 W Sunset Blvd, Echo Park; dishes $13-19; ☺8am-midnight Sun-Thu, to 1am Fri & Sat; 🛜🍴), a scrumptious vegan kitchen using local, organic ingredients, including produce from its own farm. The eatery also brews its own kombucha and beer. For a sweet, guilt-free epilogue, try the KindKreme ice cream.

❺ Stories

Wander through a mini maze of new and used literature inside **Stories** (☏213-413-3733; www.storiesla.com; 1716 W Sunset Blvd, Echo Park; ☺8am-11pm Sun-Thu, to midnight Fri & Sat; 🛜), its offerings including interesting LA-themed books. The back-end cafe comes with free wi-fi and a cute back patio.

❻ Vintage & Indie Treasure

Shop local at **Spacedust** (☏323-484-6343; https://shop.spacedustla.com; 2153 W Sunset Blvd, Echo Park; ☺noon-8pm), its small-batch wearables ranging from 70s-rocker-themed infant jumpsuits to subversive adult tees. At prized vintage store **Luxe De Ville** (p65), Oskar de la Cruz collaborates with artists, creating one-of-a-kind pieces for women and men.

Explore ◈
Highland Park

Highland Park is hot. Once plagued by gang activity, its walkable, low-rise streets have been transformed into an in-the-know hub of gentrified Craftsman homes, blog-worthy coffee shops, restaurants, bars and shops, all living side by side with throwback taquerias, barbers and Mexican grocery stores. This is not a place to tick off big-ticket sights. It is, however, the perfect place to absorb East LA at its coolest, most creative, grassroots best.

The Short List

○ **Retail Therapy (p75)** *Scoring locally made stationery and fashion, rare tomes and vinyl.*

○ **Joy (p71)** *Chowing down Taiwanese classics-with-a-twist.*

○ **Kumquat Coffee Co. (p73)** *Eavesdropping on creatives over superlative joe.*

○ **Highland Park Bowl (p71)** *Striking out at a steampunk-inspired bowling-alley bar.*

○ **Los Angeles Police Museum (p71)** *Getting the dirt on LA crime where detective Robert Grogan hunted down the Hillside Stranglers.*

Getting There & Around

Ⓜ The L Line (Gold) connects Highland Park to Downtown LA and Pasadena. Highland Park station lies one block behind N Figueroa St.

🚌 Metro Line 81 runs along N Figueroa St. Metro Line 83 services York Blvd. Both reach Downtown LA.

Neighborhood Map on p70

Highland Park

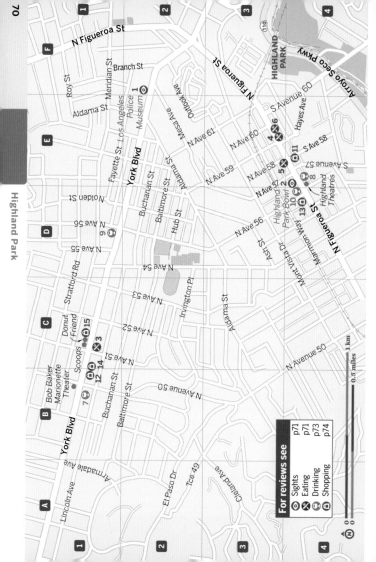

N Figueroa St

Highland Park

For reviews see

◎ Sights	p71
✕ Eating	p71
◻ Drinking	p73
◻ Shopping	p74

Lincoln Ave
Armadale Ave
York Blvd
Bob Baker Marionette Theater
Buchanan St
Baltimore St
El Paso Dr
Cleland Ave
Tce 49
N Avenue 50
N Ave 51
N Ave 52
N Ave 53
N Ave 54
N Ave 55
N Ave 56
Stratford Rd
Irvington Pl
Donut Friend
Scoops
York Blvd
Nolden St
Baltimore St
Buchanan St
Adams St
Hub St
Meridian St
Fayette St
Roy St
Aldama St
Branch St
Los Angeles Police Museum
York Blvd
Outlook Ave
Mesa Ave
N Ave 59
N Ave 58
N Ave 57
N Ave 56
N Ave 60
N Ave 61
N Ave 19
N Adams St
Ash St
Adams St
N Avenue 50
N Figueroa St
N Figueroa St
HIGHLAND PARK
Arroyo Seco Pkwy
Highland Park Bowl
Montevista Dr
Marmion Way
Highland Theatres
S Avenue 60
S Avenue 58
S Avenue 57
Hayes Ave

7
12 14
15
3
6
1
4 6
5
11
10
2
8
13

110

0   0.5 miles
0   1 km

Sights

Los Angeles Police Museum

MUSEUM

1 ◎ MAP P70, F2

Crime fighting goes under the spotlight at Police Station No 11, now better known as the Los Angeles Police Museum. Exhibits trace the history of the LAPD, from its humble beginnings in 1869 to the modern force of today. There's fascinating background on some of the city's most infamous crimes, plus a collection of historic police vehicles. Built in 1926, the handsome station itself isn't short of anecdotes, with former captives including notorious Mexican mafioso Joe 'Pegleg' Morgan. (☏323-344-9445; www.laphs.org; 6045 York Blvd, Highland Park; adult/senior/child $10/9/5; ◷10am-4pm Tue-Fri, also 9am-3pm 3rd Sat of month; P⬥; ⊟Metro Line 83, Ⓜ L Line to Highland Park)

Highland Park Bowl

BOWLING

2 ◎ MAP P70, E4

It's a bowling alley, Jim. But not as we know it. You'll be hard-pressed to find a bowling alley as stunningly original as this one, its steampunk fit-out including leather Chesterfield sofas and twin bars serving craft cocktails and beers. (☏323-257-2695; www.highlandparkbowl.com; 5621 N Figueroa St, Highland Park; bowling per lane per hr $40-70; ◷5pm-2am Mon-Fri, 11am-2am Sat & Sun; ⊟Metro Line 81, Ⓜ L Line to Highland Park)

Eating

Joy

TAIWANESE $

3 ✕ MAP P70, C1

Foodies fawn over straightforward Joy, a fast, casual eatery pumping out Taiwanese-inspired brilliance. Snap at plump, fresh wontons, flavor-packed mapo tofu or a crunchy thousand-layer pancake best jacked up with chili sauce, basil, cheese and egg. Head in early to avoid long queues. (☏323-999-7642; www.joyonyork.com; 5100 York Blvd, Highland Park; dishes $4-12; ◷noon-10pm; ✦⬥; ⊟Metro Line 83, DASH Highland Park/Eagle Rock Route)

Kitchen Mouse

VEGETARIAN $

4 ✕ MAP P70, E3

Adorned with sidewalk tables and freshly picked flowers, homey Kitchen Mouse is Highland Park's favorite herbivore. Everyone from alt-fashion bloggers to middle-class couples flock here for generous, mood-lifting vegan and vegetarian dishes, whether it's sesame brown-rice cakes with crispy oyster mushrooms or avocado TLT, the latter a blissful combo of avocado, maple-tempeh bacon, cherry tomatoes and Dijon aioli. Good coffee, too. (☏323-259-9555; www.kitchenmousela.com; 5904 N Figueroa St, Highland Park; dishes $11-15; ◷8am-4pm Mon-Fri, 7am-4pm Sat & Sun; ��✦⬥; ⊟Metro Line 81, DASH Highland Park/Eagle Rock Route, Ⓜ L Line to Highland Park)

Highland Park for Sweet Tooths

Highland Park's sugar highs are among LA's best. Don't miss the wildly creative **Donut Friend** (Map p70, C1; ☑213-908-2745; www.donutfriend.com; 5107 York Blvd, Highland Park; donuts from $2.30; ◷7am-10pm Sun-Thu, to midnight Fri & Sat; ⚙; ⊠Metro Line 83, DASH Highland Park/Eagle Rock Route), where holed treats are sprinkled with coconut bacon, stuffed with vegan cream cheese and fresh basil or drizzled in glazes such as matcha tea and maple. For an icy revelation, neighboring **Scoops** (Map p70, C1; ☑323-906-2649; 5105 York St, Highland Park; one scoop $5.50, pints $9.50; ◷2-9pm Mon-Thu, 1-10pm Fri & Sat, to 8pm Sun; ⚑⚙; ⊠Metro Line 83, DASH Highland Park/Eagle Rock Route) serves small-batch, artisan ice cream, offered in out-of-the-box flavors like black currant lavender.

Cafe Birdie
MODERN AMERICAN $$

5 🍴 MAP P70, E3

Market-fresh ingredients drive elevated comfort dishes at this slinky Highland Park hot spot, complete with marble-topped bar and an intimate, light-strung back patio. Cleanse the palate with one of the delicate, seasonal salads before sinking your teeth into the standout Moroccan-spiced fried chicken. Birdie's pasta dishes and creative cocktails are equally gorgeous. (☑323-739-6928; www.cafebirdiela.com; 5631 N Figueroa St, Highland Park; dinner mains $17-23; ◷5:30-10pm Mon-Thu, to 11pm Fri, 10am-2:30pm & 5-11pm Sat, 10am-2:30pm & 5-10pm Sun; ⚑; ⊠Metro Line 81, Ⓜ L Line to Highland Park)

Triple Beam Pizza
PIZZA $

6 🍴 MAP P70, E3

Triple Beam's Roman-style pizza by the slice is superb. The base is crisp and the rotating options inspired: picture roasted acorn squash with mozzarella, fontina, cream, honey and *piccantissimo* (Umbrian spice blend) or piquillo peppers matched with kalamata olives, capers, arugula and tomato sauce. Simply line up, indicate how big a slice you'd like and devour it on the back patio. (www.triplebeampizza.com; 5918 N Figueroa St, Highland Park; pizza per oz from $0.80; ◷noon-10pm Sun-Thu, to 11pm Fri & Sat; ⧉⚑⚙; ⊠Metro Line 81, DASH Highland Park/Eagle Rock Route, Ⓜ L Line to Highland Park)

Drinking

Kumquat Coffee Co. COFFEE

7 🖉 MAP P70, B1

Quite possibly *the* best Third-Wave coffee shop in LA, this welcoming, minimalist space brews consistently superb joe with meticulous attention to detail. Both home-grown and international micro-roasteries are rotated, including the odd cult-status roaster from caffeine-obsessed Melbourne, Australia. More unusual options here include a popular *hojicha* (green tea) latte. (www.kumquatcoffee.com; 4936 York Blvd, Highland Park; 🕘7am-5pm; 🛜💺; 🚉 Metro Line 83, DASH Highland Park/Eagle Rock Route)

ETA COCKTAIL BAR

8 🖉 MAP P70, E4

One of the city's top cocktail dens, intimate ETA serves innovative, complex libations that might include a Hot and Heavy, an out-of-the-box mix of tequila blanco, Aperol, watermelon, bitters, agave, lime and sweet-and-spicy salt. The mural you're looking at is by local artist Johnny Tarajosu, while the popular happy hour (until 8pm daily) will have you slurping on $1 oysters. (📞216-571-6301; www.facebook.com/ETAHLP; 5630 N Figueroa St, Highland Park; 🕘5pm-1am Mon-Thu, to 2am Fri, 3pm-2am Sat, 3-8pm Sun; 🚉 Metro Line 81, Ⓜ L Line to Highland Park)

Holcomb WINE BAR

9 🖉 MAP P70, D1

When it comes to vino, neighborly Holcomb offers more twists and turns than a Hitchcock flick. Should you quaff a sparkling orange pét-nat from Italy's Emilia-Romagna, a vidiano from Greece or perhaps a dolcetto from Oregon's Eola-Amity Hills? Clued-in barkeeps will happily guide you towards your new favorite drop, always best paired with Holcomb's divine pork-rillettes sandwich or house-cured duck. (5535 York Blvd, Highland Park; 🕘5pm-midnight Sun-Thu, to 1am Fri & Sat; 🚉 Metro Line 83)

Donut Friend

DAVID MCNEW/AFP/GETTY IMAGES ©

Gold Line
BAR

10 ⊖ MAP P70, D4

Vinyl is king at mellow hi-fi bar Gold Line. Its hefty record collection includes rare discs from bar co-founder, DJ/music producer Peanut Butter Wolf. Let the good vibes flow while sipping a top-notch drink, whether it be a highball cocktail, rare mezcal or whiskey, or glass of tangy natural wine. Happy hour (5pm to 7pm) includes great-value $8 cocktails. (www.facebook.com/goldlinebar; 5607 N Figueroa St, Highland Park; ⊙5pm-midnight Mon-Thu, to 2am Fri, 2pm-2am Sat, to midnight Sun; 🛜; 🚊Metro Line 81, Ⓜ️L Line to Highland Park)

Bob Baker Marionette Theater

LUCY NICHOLSON/ALAMY STOCK PHOTO ©

Shopping

Sunbeam Vintage
VINTAGE

11 🔒 MAP P70, E4

Nirvana for fans of mid-century-modern design, Sunbeam Vintage stocks a fabulous collection of retro furniture and homewares. Dive in for pineapple-shaped brass lamps, bar carts, elegant velvet armchairs, timber side tables, metallic art and even giant metal letters from old marquees. (📞323-908-9743; www.sunbeamvintage.com; 106 S Ave 58, Highland Park; ⊙10am-6pm; 🚊Metro Line 81, DASH Highland Park/Eagle Rock Route, Ⓜ️L Line to Highland Park)

Big Bud Press
FASHION & ACCESSORIES

12 🔒 MAP P70, B1

At the end of the rainbow lies this explosion of Technicolor grooviness. Designed and made in LA, its size-inclusive, unisex booty includes 70s-inspired jumpsuits in juicy hues like 'creamsicle orange' and 'flamingo pink,' retro striped tees and outrageous power suits that would make Marcia Brady squeal. High-profile collaborators have included Lisa Hanawalt, production designer/producer of Netflix animated series *BoJack Horseman*. (www.bigbudpress.com; 5028 York Blvd, Highland Park; ⊙noon-7pm Mon & Wed-Fri, 11am-6pm Sat & Sun; 🚊Metro Line 83, DASH Highland Park/Eagle Rock Route)

Avalon Vintage   VINTAGE

13 🔒 MAP P70, D4

One of the best-loved consignment stores in LA, known for stocking more unusual retro frocks and outfits. It's hardly surprising since store owner Carmen Hawk was Milla Jovovich's former design partner at Jovovich-Hawk. You'll also find an eclectic collection of old vinyl records, with offerings including classic rock and pop, soul, jazz and reggae. (☎ 323-309-7717; www.facebook.com/avalonrecords; 106 N Ave 56, Highland Park; ⏱ 1-8pm Tue-Sun; 🚇 Metro Line 81, DASH Highland Park/Eagle Rock Route; Ⓜ L Line to Highland Park)

Shorthand   STATIONERY

14 🔒 MAP P70, C1

Oh-so-pretty Shorthand stocks adorable cards and delightful stationery, including items made by in-house letterpress printer Iron Curtain Press. You'll also find a range of pens, pencils and markers, pencil cases, sticky notes and other design-savvy desk essentials. We love the graphic-themed prints of LA and California, not to mention the supercute pins, embroidered patches and high-quality, locally made soy-wax candles. (☎ 323-642-9039; www.shopshorthand.com; 5030 York Blvd, Highland Park; ⏱ 11am-7pm; 🚇 Metro Line 83, DASH Highland Park/Eagle Rock Route)

Cheap Flicks & Vintage Puppets

While there's nothing fancy about **Highland Theatres** (Map p70, E4; ☎ 323-256-6383; www.highlandtheatres.com; 5604 N Figueroa St, Highland Park; ♿; 🚇 Metro Line 81, DASH Highland Park/Eagle Rock Route, Ⓜ L Line to Highland Park), tickets at this retro triplex are a bargain $7 before 6pm. Over on York St, a former vaudeville theater is home to the equally loved **Bob Baker Marionette Theater** (Map p70, B1; ☎ 213-250-9995; www.bobbakermarionettetheater.com; 4949 York Blvd, Highland Park; ♿; 🚇 Metro Line 83, DASH Highland Park/Eagle Rock Route), LA's oldest children's theater company.

Permanent Records   MUSIC

15 🔒 MAP P70, C1

Permanent's black crates are jammed with new and used vinyl. The Chicago import pays decent money for vinyl, which translates into a strong offering of collectable and limited-edition discs. Fortes include garage, psych and hard rock, as well as some deliciously obscure treasures. (☎ 323-739-6141; www.permanentrecordsla.com; 5123 York Blvd, Highland Park; ⏱ noon-8pm; 🚇 Metro Line 83, DASH Highland Park/Eagle Rock Route)

Explore

West Hollywood & Beverly Hills

LA rainbows end in West Hollywood (WeHo), an independent city with way more punch (and unbridled revelry) than its 1.9-sq-mile frame might suggest. Packed with famous comedy clubs, legendary showbiz hotels and trendy, celeb-frequented restaurants and boutiques, it's also the city's gay heartland. To the west is salubrious Beverly Hills, home to high-end shopping strip Rodeo Drive and swanky bistros filled with power-lunching film execs.

The Short List

o **Frederick R Weisman Art Foundation (p80)** *Eyeing up pop art in a rich-and-famous mansion.*

o **Polo Lounge (p84)** *Enjoying gin martinis and Hollywood anecdotes at Beverly Hills' most famous drinking hole.*

o **Museum of Tolerance (p80)** *Reflecting on light, darkness and the Holocaust.*

o **Abbey (p86)** *Starting (and ending) here on a rainbow-colored bar crawl of Boystown.*

o **Bikes & Hikes LA (p82)** *Getting LA-fit on a 32-mile sightseeing ride.*

Getting There & Around

🚌 Metro Lines 2 and 302 connect Sunset Blvd in West Hollywood to Westwood, Hollywood, Silver Lake, Echo Park and Downtown LA. Metro Lines 4 and 704 run along Santa Monica Blvd in West Hollywood and Beverly Hills, also reaching Hollywood, Silver Lake, Echo Park and Downtown LA.

Neighborhood Map on p78

Abbey (p86) VALERIE MACON/AFP/GETTY IMAGES ©

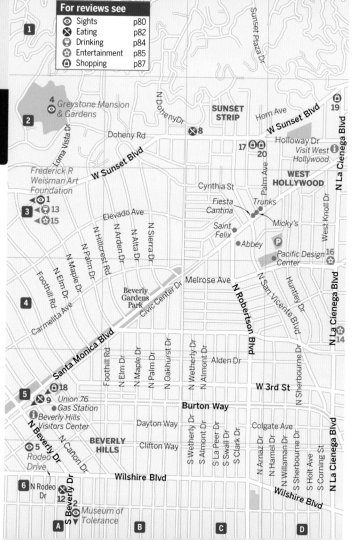

For reviews see

- 👁 Sights p80
- ✖ Eating p82
- 🍷 Drinking p84
- ⭐ Entertainment p85
- 🛍 Shopping p87

1

2

Greystone Mansion & Gardens

4

Loma Vista Dr

Sunset Plaza Dr

N Doheny Dr

SUNSET STRIP

Horn Ave

W Sunset Blvd

Doheny Rd

Doheny Rd

8

17 20

Holloway Dr

Visit West Hollywood

Palm Ave

WEST HOLLYWOOD

N La Cienega Blvd

19

W Sunset Blvd

Frederick R Weisman Art Foundation

1
13
15

3

Cynthia St

Fiesta Cantina

Trunks

Saint Felix

Micky's

Abbey

Elevado Ave

N Hillcrest Rd

N Arden Dr

N Sierra Dr

West Knoll Dr

Pacific Design Center

16

Beverly Gardens Park

Melrose Ave

Civic Center Dr

N San Vicente Blvd

Huntley Dr

N Robertson Blvd

N La Cienega Blvd

14

4

Foothill Rd

N Elm Dr

N Maple Dr

N Palm Dr

Carmelita Ave

Santa Monica Blvd

Foothill Rd

N Elm Dr

N Maple Dr

N Palm Dr

N Oakhurst Dr

N Wetherly Dr

N Almont Dr

Alden Dr

N Sherbourne Dr

W 3rd St

5

18

9

Union 76 Gas Station

Beverly Hills Visitors Center

Burton Way

Dayton Way

S Wetherly Dr

S Almont Dr

S La Peer Dr

S Swall Dr

S Clark Dr

Colgate Ave

N Arnaz Dr

N Hamel Dr

N Willaman Dr

N La Cienega Blvd

BEVERLY HILLS

5

Rodeo Drive

N Beverly Dr

N Cañon Dr

Clifton Way

Wilshire Blvd

S Holt Ave

S Corning St

6

N Rodeo Dr

12

S Beverly Dr

Museum of Tolerance

Wilshire Blvd

1 km
0.5 miles

E **F** **G** **H**

N

1

W Sunset Blvd

Laugh Factory

N Kings Rd

De Longpre Ave

Comedy Store

William S Hart Park

Fountain Ave

N Crescent Heights Blvd

N Orange Grove Ave

N Ogden Dr

N Genesee Ave

N Vista St

N Martel Ave

N Flores St

WEST HOLLYWOOD

Hampton Ave

Plummer Park

2

Lexington Ave

Norton Ave

Norton Ave

7 ☒

Santa Monica Blvd

Santa Monica Blvd

☒ Bikes &
6 Hikes LA

N Kings Rd

N Sweetzer Ave

Romaine St

N Laurel Ave

N Edinburgh Ave

N Hayworth Ave

N Fairfax Ave

N Orange Grove Ave

N Ogden Dr

N Genesee Ave

N Curson Ave

N Sierra Bonita Ave

Poinsettia Recreation Center

Willoughby St

3 ☒
Schindler House

Waring Ave

3

Melrose Ave

Groundlings

☒ Improv

Melrose Ave

BEVERLY CENTER DISTRICT

Clinton St

Clinton St

Rosewood Ave

Rosewood Ave

4

N Fairfax Ave

N Spaulding Ave

N Stanley Ave

N Curson Ave

N Gardner St

N Vista St

N Martel Ave

N Fuller Ave

Oakwood Ave

N Ogden Dr

Beverly Blvd

FAIRFAX DISTRICT

11 ☒

Beverly Blvd

S Edinburgh Ave

W 1st St

P

The Grove Dr

MID-CITY

5

W 3rd St

☒**10**

S Orlando Ave

S Sweetzer Ave

The Grove

Pan Pacific Park

S Gardner St

S Vista St

S Martel Ave

S Fuller Ave

Colgate Ave

W 3rd St

S Fairfax Ave

ColgateAve

6

S Curson Ave

W 6th St

E **F** **G** **H**

Sights

Frederick R Weisman Art Foundation
MUSEUM

1  MAP P78, A3

The late entrepreneur and philanthropist Frederick R Weisman had an insatiable passion for art, a fact confirmed when touring his former Holmby Hills home. From floor to ceiling, the mansion (and its manicured grounds) bursts with extraordinary works from visionaries such as Picasso, Kandinsky, Miró, Magritte, Rothko, Warhol, Rauschenberg and Ruscha. There's even a motorcycle painted by Keith Haring. Tours should be reserved at least a few days ahead. (☏310-277-5321; www.weismanfoundation.org; 265 N Carolwood Dr, Holmby Hills; admission free; ⏱1¾hr guided tours 10:30am & 2pm Mon-Fri, by appointment only; ☐Metro Lines 2, 302)

Museum of Tolerance
MUSEUM

2  MAP P78, A6

Run by the Simon Wiesenthal Center, this powerful, deeply moving museum uses interactive technology to engage visitors in discussion and contemplation around racism and bigotry. Particular focus is given to the Holocaust, with a major basement exhibition that examines the social, political and economic conditions that led to the Holocaust as well as the experience of the millions persecuted. On the museum's 2nd floor, another major exhibition offers an intimate look into the life and impact of Anne Frank.

Rodeo Drive

FRANK FELL MEDIA/SHUTTERSTOCK ©

The third Tuesday of the month is free for general admission (does not include Anne Frank exhibit). (☏reservations 310-772-2505; www. museumoftolerance.com; 9786 W Pico Blvd; adult/senior & student/child $15.50/12.50/11.50, Anne Frank Exhibit $15.50/13.50/12.50; ◷10am-5pm Sun-Wed & Fri, to 9.30pm Thu Apr-Oct, 10am-5pm Sun-Wed, to 9.30pm Thu, to 3.30pm Fri Nov-Mar; 🅿🚻; 🚌Big Blue Bus Line 7)

Schindler House   ARCHITECTURE

3 ◉ MAP P78, E3

The former home and studio of Vienna-born architect Rudolph Schindler (1887–1953) offers a fine primer on the modernist elements that so greatly influenced mid-century California architecture. The open floor plan, flat roof and glass sliding doors, while considered avant-garde back in the 1920s, all became design staples after WWII. (☏323-651-1510; www. makcenter.org; 835 N Kings Rd, West Hollywood; adult/senior & student/ under 12 $10/7/free, 4-6pm Fri free; ◷11am-6pm Wed-Sun; 🚌Metro Lines 4, 10, 704, DASH Fairfax Route)

Greystone Mansion & Gardens   NOTABLE BUILDING

4 ◉ MAP P78, A2

Featured in countless TV shows and movies (including *The Big Lebowski*), this 1927 Tudor Revival mansion was designed by Hoover Dam architect Gordon Bernie Kaufmann. It was a generous gift from oil tycoon Edward L Doheny to his son Ned and his family. In 1929 the oil heir was found dead along with his male secretary in an alleged murder-suicide – a mystery that remains unsolved to this day.

While the elegant grounds – which offer commanding views of LA – are accessible year round, the mansion itself is only open for special events and two-hour guided tours ($20). The latter usually take place at 10am and 2pm on the first Saturday of the month January through April, as well as on the first Sunday of the month in March and April. (☏310-285-6830; www.beverlyhills.org/departments/ communityservices/cityparks; 905 Loma Vista Dr, Beverly Hills; admission free; ◷10am-6pm mid-Mar–Oct, to 5pm Nov–mid-Mar; 🅿)

Rodeo Drive   STREET

5 ◉ MAP P78, A6

It might be pricey and unapologetically pretentious, but no trip to LA would be complete without a saunter along Rodeo Dr, the famous three-block ribbon of style where sample-size fembots browse for Gucci and Dior. Fashion retailer Fred Hayman opened the strip's first luxury boutique – Giorgio Beverly Hills – at number 273 back in 1961. Famed for its striped white-and-yellow awning, the store allowed its well-heeled clients to sip cocktails while shopping and have their purchases home delivered in a Rolls-Royce. (🚌Metro Lines 4, 14, 16, 37, 316, 704)

Architectural Landmarks

West Hollywood, Beverly Hills and neighboring Century City claim numerous important architectural landmarks. Argentinian architect César Pelli (designer of Kuala Lumpur's Petronas Towers) is the mastermind behind the **Pacific Design Center** (PDC; Map p78, D3; www.pacificdesigncenter.com; 8687 Melrose Ave, West Hollywood; ⏰9am-5pm Mon-Fri; 🚇Metro Lines 4, 10, 704). Built in stages between 1975 and 2012, its three glass buildings – one each in red, green and blue – resemble giant, geometric toys. Further west, the **Union 76 Gas Station** (Map p78, A5; cnr Crescent Dr & S Santa Monica Blvd, Beverly Hills; 🚇Metro Lines 4, 14, 16, 37, 316, 704) is a fine example of Googie architecture, a mid-century, SoCal style informed by the era's burgeoning space industry and car culture. Built in 1965, its acclaimed architect Gin Wong had originally envisaged it as part of his LAX airport masterplan. Further west still is the 44-story **Century Plaza Towers**. Its architect, Minoru Yamasaki, also designed New York's ill-fated Twin Towers.

Bikes & Hikes LA

OUTDOORS

6 🔘 MAP P78, F2

This WeHo-based outfit rents bikes and offers scheduled cycling tours of Hollywood and Beverly Hills, as well as the signature 32-mile 'LA in a Day' ($139) for fit cyclists, taking in celebrity homes, swank shopping streets, inspiring architecture and the Pacific. Hiking tours venture around Griffith Park (including awesome Hollywood Sign selfies) on a light-to-moderate, family-friendly hike. Custom tours are also available. (☎323-796-8555; www.bikesandhikesla.com; 8250 Santa Monica Blvd, West Hollywood; guided bike tours from $55, hike tours $35, bike rentals per day from $32; 🚴; 🚇Metro Lines 4, 704)

Eating

Connie & Ted's

SEAFOOD $$

7 🍴 MAP P78, F2

Acclaimed chef Michael Cimarusti is behind this buzzing, homely take on the New England seafood shack. Freshness and sustainability underscore the offerings, with up to a dozen oyster varieties at the raw bar, as well as superb, authentic renditions of northeast classics such as lobster rolls, clam cakes, chowder and steamers. (☎323-848-2722; www.connieandteds.com; 8171 Santa Monica Blvd, West Hollywood; mains $15-29; ⏰4-10pm Mon & Tue, 11:30am-10pm Wed & Thu, to 11pm Fri, 10am-11pm Sat, to 10pm Sun; 🅿; 🚇Metro Lines 4, 218)

Night + Market
THAI $

8 MAP P78, C2

Fun, bright Night + Market pumps out outstanding Thai street food and Thai-inspired hybrids like a must-try fried-chicken sandwich with papaya slaw. Other standouts include *peek gai hey-ha* (sweet battered wings), *nam khao tod* (crispy rice salad with soured pork) and rich, fragrant *panang en neua* (beef short-rib curry). Then there's the pad Thai, mercifully less sweet than most LA versions. Book ahead. (310-275-9724; www.nightmarketla.com; 9043 W Sunset Blvd, West Hollywood; dishes $8-16; 11:30am-2:30pm Tue-Thu & 5-10:30pm Tue-Sun; P; Metro Line 2)

Eataly LA
FOOD HALL

9 MAP P78, A5

Part of Westfield Century City, the LA branch of this Italian gastronomic Disneyland features a dedicated wine store, bakery, cheese, charcuterie and fresh produce sections, plus both quick-service counters and sit-down restaurants peddling everything from cannoli and wood-fired pizzas to proper pasta and responsibly sourced seafood dishes. If you love your gin, grab a pre-dinner G&T at its rooftop restaurant-bar **Terra** (11:30am-2:30pm & 5-10pm Mon-Thu, 10:30am-2:30pm Sat & Sun & 5-10:30pm Fri & Sat, 5-9:30pm Sun; P), but dine at the better-value Eataly options downstairs. (213-310-8000; www.eataly.com/us_en/stores/los-angeles; 10250 Santa Monica Blvd, Westfield Century City; pizzas $13-29, pasta $14-39, fish mains $28; 8am-10pm Sun-Thu, to 11pm Fri & Sat, individual eateries vary; P; Metro Lines 4, 16, 28, 316, 704, 728, Big Blue Bus Line 5)

Slab
BARBECUE $$

10 MAP P78, F5

After perfecting Texas-style BBQ in his backyard, pitmaster Burt Bakman opened this little timber-clad ode to Lone Star–style meats (that's Burt in the photographs). Top billing goes to the smoky, melt-in-your-mouth spare ribs, the sticky-and-sweet Tony's baby back ribs and the beautifully seasoned brisket. Sauces and sides are made from scratch, from the mac 'n' cheese to the collard greens and frito pie. (310-855-7184; www.slabbarbecue.com; 8136 W 3rd St; brisket per lb $28, half/whole ribs $16/29; 11am-9pm; ; Metro Lines 16, 17, 218)

Escuela Taqueria
MEXICAN $

11 MAP P78, G4

An affordable, new-school taqueria with top-notch ingredients. Highlights include the pork-rib tacos, smashingly paired with a housemade sweet-chili sauce. While tacos and burritos dominate the menu, don't overlook the *tinga tostada*, topped with a moreish combo of stewed chicken, refried beans and sour cream. And while the place doesn't sell alcohol, you can bring your own for a small fee.

(☎323-932-6178; www.escuelataque
ria.com; 7615 Beverly Blvd, Mid-City;
tacos & burritos $4-13; ⌚11am-11pm;
🚇Metro Lines 14, 37)

Chaumont Bakery & Cafe

CAFE $

12 ✖ MAP P78, A6

Owned by a true-*bleu* French
couple, this pretty patisserie
serves fabulous croissants (opt
for the almond version), *pain au
chocolat* and other too-cute-to-eat
treats, from fruit-topped tarts to
eclairs. For something a little more
substantial, devour the flawless
Gruyère and mushroom omelet,
the French toast or the smoked-
salmon and poached-egg crois-
sant. *Très bon!* (☎310-550-5510;
143 S Beverly Dr, Beverly Hills; pastries

from $3, dishes $12-21; ⌚6:30am-
6:30pm Mon-Thu, to 4pm Fri & Sat,
7:30am-2pm Sun; 🚼🚻; 🚇Metro
Lines 14, 37)

Drinking

Polo Lounge

COCKTAIL BAR

13 🍸 MAP P78, A3

For a classic LA experience, dress
up and swill evening martinis in
the Beverly Hills Hotel's legendary bar. Charlie Chaplin had a
standing lunch reservation at
booth 1 and it was here that HR
Haldeman and John Ehrlichman
learned of the Watergate break-in
in 1972. There's a popular (albeit
overrated) Sunday jazz brunch
($95). Don't miss the historical
photographs of the hotel, hung

Chaumont Bakery & Cafe

both inside the venue and at its entrance. (☎310-887-2777; www.dorchestercollection.com/en/los-angeles/the-beverly-hills-hotel; Beverly Hills Hotel, 9641 Sunset Blvd, Beverly Hills; ⏱7am-1:30am; 🛜; 🚇Metro Lines 2, 302)

Roger Room COCKTAIL BAR

Cramped but cool; too cool even to have a sign out front. When handcrafted, throwback cocktails first migrated west and south from New York and San Fran, they landed here (see 14 ⭐ Map p78, D4), amid velvet booths and well-dressed, mustachioed bartenders. Best drinks in the neighborhood? You bet. (☎310-854-1300; www.therogerroom.com; 370 N La Cienega Blvd, Mid-City; ⏱6pm-2am Mon-Fri, 7pm-2am Sat, 8pm-2am Sun; 🚇Metro Lines 14, 105, 705, DASH Fairfax Route)

Entertainment

Largo at the Coronet COMEDY

14 ⭐ MAP P78, D4

Ever since its early days on Fairfax Ave, Largo has been progenitor of high-minded pop culture (it nurtured Zach Galifianakis to stardom). Now part of the Coronet Theatre complex, it features edgy comedy – we're talking Nick Offerman, Margaret Cho and Bo Burnham – as well as nourishing night music from the likes of singer-songwriter Jon Brion. (☎310-855-0350; www.largo-la.com; 366 N La Cienega Blvd, Mid-City; 🚇Metro Lines 14, 37)

Yuk it Up

Some of America's top comics got their feet wet at WeHo's comedy clubs.

The **Comedy Store** (Map p78, E1; ☎323-650-6268; www.thecomedystore.com; 8433 W Sunset Blvd, West Hollywood; 🛜; 🚇Metro Line 2) has been a thing since it brought in hot young comics such as Robin Williams and David Letterman.

The Marx Brothers kept offices at the **Laugh Factory** (Map p78, F1; ☎323-656-1336; www.laughfactory.com; 8001 W Sunset Blvd; 🚇Metro Line 2) and it still gets some big names.

The **Groundlings** (p102) launched Kathy Griffin, among others, while the **Improv** (Map p78, F3; ☎323-651-2583; www.improv.com; 8162 Melrose Ave, Mid-City; 🚇Metro Line 10) launched countless stand-ups, including Jerry Seinfeld and Ellen DeGeneres.

Vibrato Grill Bar JAZZ

15 ⭐ MAP P78, A3

You can thank Grammy Award–winning jazz legend Herb Alpert for the standout acoustics here. After all, he designed the elegant, romantic spot. A restaurant and jazz club in one, it serves up six nights of stellar acts, from Cali standouts like the Freddie Ravel Trio to international guests such as

WeHo,
End of the Rainbow

West Hollywood is simply is one of the world's top spots for gay nightlife, with dozens of shops, restaurants and nightspots all along Santa Monica Blvd; the highest concentration is between Robertson Blvd and Palm Dr. The **Abbey** (Map p78, C3; ☎310-289-8410; www.theabbeyweho.com; 692 N Robertson Blvd, West Hollywood; ⏰11am-2am Mon-Thu, 10am-2am Fri, 9am-2am Sat & Sun; 🛜; 🚇Metro Lines 4, 704) has been called the world's best gay bar, with a multitude of polished indoor-outdoor spaces. **Saint Felix** (Map p78, C3; ☎310-275-4428; www.facebook.com/saintfelixwesthollywood; 8945 Santa Monica Blvd; ⏰4pm-2am Mon-Sat, 2pm-2am Sun; 🛜; 🚇Metro Lines 4, 704) is great for happy hour, lacking the scene-in-overdrive feel of some of its neighbors. **Micky's** (Map p78, C3; ☎310-657-1176; www.mickys.com; 8857 Santa Monica Blvd, West Hollywood; ⏰5pm-2am Mon-Thu, to 4am Fri, 3pm-4am Sat, 2pm-2am Sun; 🛜; 🚇Metro Lines 4, 704) is a quintessential WeHo dance club, with go-go boys and plenty of eye candy, while hedonistic **Fiesta Cantina** (Map p78, C3; ☎310-652-8865; www.fiestacantina.net; 8865 Santa Monica Blvd, West Hollywood; ⏰noon-2am; 🛜; 🚇Metro Lines 4, 704) is raucous thanks to extra-long happy hours and all-you-can-eat Taco Tuesdays. The crowd skews somewhat older at **Trunks** (Map p78, C3; ☎310-652-1015; www.west.hollywood.trunksbar.com; 8809 Santa Monica Blvd, West Hollywood; ⏰1pm-2am; 🛜; Ⓜ Metro Lines 4, 704), a brick-house, low-lit dive that's more down to earth than most in WeHo (and that can be a very good thing).

Maria Elena Infantino. Reservations (and smart outfits) are highly recommended. (☎310-474-9400; www.vibratogrilljazz.com; 2930 Beverly Glen Circle, Bel Air; ⏰5-11pm Tue-Sun)

Melrose
Rooftop Theatre   OUTDOOR CINEMA

16 ⭐ MAP P78, D3

From mid-April to December, Melrose Rooftop Theatre takes over the rooftop at restaurant-bar EP & LP. Movies screen at sundown from Sunday to Thursday, with an eclectic mix of recent releases and modern classics like *Pulp Fiction* and *Dirty Dancing*. Wireless headsets and bean bags are provided, with decent cocktails on standby. Tickets sell out quickly; reserve a week or two ahead. (☎310-855-9955; www.melrserooftoptheatre.com; 603 N La Cienega Blvd, West Hollywood; tickets from $27.50; ⏰mid-Apr–Dec; 🚇Metro Lines 10, 105)

Shopping

Mystery Pier Books BOOKS

17 🔒 MAP P78, C2

The charming Louis and Harvey have no shortage of fans (including famous ones) thanks to their remarkable WeHo bookstore. Famed for stocking signed shooting scripts from blockbusters, it also sells rare and obscure 1st editions, from Shakespeare ($3500 to $9000) and Salinger ($10,000) to JK Rowling ($30,000 and up). (📞310-657-5557; www.mysterypier books.com; 8826 W Sunset Blvd, West Hollywood; ⏰11am-6pm Mon-Sat, noon-5pm Sun; 🚇Metro Lines 2, 302)

Westfield Century City MALL

18 🔒 MAP P78, A5

This is West LA's best mall, a buzzing, sun-dappled, indoor-outdoor wonderland of midrange and high-end retail. Major draws include Italian gourmet temple Eataly LA (p83), impressive branches of department-store giants Bloomingdale's, Macy's *and* Nordstrom, plus a state-of-the-art, 15-screen AMC multiplex. When pooped, refuel at one of the quality restaurants or in the food court, home to outposts of numerous top LA casual eateries. (📞310-277-3898; www.westfield.com/centurycity; 10250 Santa Monica Blvd, Century City; ⏰10am-9pm Mon-Sat, 11am-7pm Sun, individual restaurant and movie theater hours vary; 📶👥; 🚇Metro Lines 4, 16, 28, 316, 704, 728, Big Blue Bus Line 5)

Fred Segal FASHION & ACCESSORIES

19 🔒 MAP P78, D2

No LA shopping trip is complete without a stop at Fred's. This is its flagship store, 21,000-sq-ft of chic, Cali-casual threads, accessories, beauty products and homewares hip enough for cashed-up celebs. The space also hosts regular product drops, trunk shows and live music. Alas, the only time you'll see bargains (sort of) is during the summer and January sales. (📞310-432-0560; www.fredsegal.com; 8500 Sunset Blvd, West Hollywood; ⏰10am-7pm Mon-Sat, 11am-6pm Sun; 🚇Metro Lines 2, 302)

Book Soup BOOKS

20 🔒 MAP P78, C2

This indie veteran has been feeding bookworms since 1975. It's packed with over 60,000 titles, including entertainment, travel, feminist and queer studies, not to mention eclectic, edgy and LA-based fiction. Collectors will find signed book copies and there's a great selection of magazines. Regular in-store author events are known to feature heavyweights of the publishing and entertainment worlds. (📞310-659-3110; www.book soup.com; 8818 W Sunset Blvd, West Hollywood; ⏰9am-10pm Mon-Sat, to 7pm Sun; 🚇Metro Lines 2, 302)

Top Experience 📷
Admire the Art and Architecture of the Getty Center

Straddling a hilltop in the Santa Monica Mountains, the $1.3-billion Getty Center offers an irresistible feast of art, design and botanical beauty. Ponder the myths and landscapes of Dossi, Van Gogh and Cézanne, and gaze out over the City of Angels and kick back in a verdant wonderland of gurgling water, lush lawns and world-famous sculptures.

📞 310-440-7300
www.getty.edu
off I-405 Fwy
admission free
🕐 10am-5:30pm Tue-Fri & Sun, to 9pm Sat
🅿️ 🚻
🚌 Metro Lines 234, 734

Collections

Although not everyone is captivated by the Getty's collection of European art, which spans the 17th to the 20th centuries, there are genuine treasures. Seek out Gentileschi's *Danaë and the Shower of Gold* and Rembrandt's self-portrait *Rembrandt Laughing* in the east pavilion, and Van Gogh's *Irises*, Monet's *Wheatstacks, Snow Effect, Morning*, Manet's *Jeanne (Spring)* and Turner's *Modern Rome – Campo Vaccino* in the west pavilion. The south pavilion's outdoor terrace is home to Marino Marini's excitable bronze *Angel of the Citadel*, originally owned by Hollywood producer Ray Stark of *Steel Magnolias* fame, while the grounds themselves are studded with prized sculptures, including three works by Henry Moore.

Architecture & Gardens

As famous for its built form as it is for its art, the Getty Center originates from the drawing board of Pritzker Prize–winning architect Richard Meier. Completed in 1997, the complex is clad in 16,000 tons of cleft-cut travertine sourced from the same Italian quarry used to construct Rome's ancient Colosseum. Look closely and you'll spot ancient, fossilized shells, fish and foliage.

Events

Aside from free tours throughout the day, the Getty360 initiative oversees a wide range of mostly free events, including talks, symposia and curated film screenings. Some require reservations, though standby tickets are often available. On Saturday evenings from May to September, the center hosts **Off the 405** (admission free; ⏱6-9pm Sat), a popular series featuring tremendous progressive pop and world-music acts in the Getty courtyard.

★ **Top Tips**

○ Visit early morning or mid-afternoon. Sunsets create a remarkable alchemy of light and shadow and are especially magical in winter. Saturday nights are usually not too crowded and parking is $15 after 3pm.

○ Grab a *Today at the Getty* leaflet from the information desk in the lobby, which lists the day's tours and special events.

○ Free and worthy audio guides are also available in the lobby. Bring photo ID; preferably a driver's license, rather than a passport.

✕ **Take a Break**

The Getty Center is home to a fine-dining modern American restaurant and two casual cafes. While all three are satisfactory, none are especially outstanding, so consider bringing a picnic lunch to enjoy on the grounds instead.

Explore
Miracle Mile
& Mid-City

Mid-City may not have the flirtatious rep of West Hollywood to the north, nor the fabled glamor of Beverly Hills to the west, but these gridded streets claim some of LA's top cultural and retail assets. It's here that you'll find the 'Miracle Mile' and its string of blockbuster museums, the Orthodox-Jewish-meets-hipster Fairfax district and world-famous Melrose Ave, as much a bastion of pop culture as it is a coveted shopping strip.

The Short List

○ *Academy Museum of Motion Pictures (p92)* Celebrating cinema at an Oscar-worthy film museum.

○ *Los Angeles County Museum of Art (p94)* Diving into an eclectic feast of top-tier artworks.

○ *Petersen Automotive Museum (p98)* Purring over Hollywood-famous wheels.

○ *Melrose Avenue (p102)* Shop-hopping and celebrity-spotting on a cult-status strip.

○ *Groundlings (p102)* Splitting your sides at the improv school that churned out Will Ferrell.

Getting There & Around

🚌 Metro Line 10 runs along Melrose Ave, Metro Line 14 serves Beverly Blvd and both Metro Lines 217 and 218 connect the two thoroughfares to Wilshire Blvd further south. The DASH Fairfax Route runs along La Cienega Blvd, Melrose Ave, Fairfax Ave, 3rd St and Wilshire Blvd.

Neighborhood Map on p96

Petersen Automotive Museum (p98) ARCHITECTS: KPF: IMAGE: DEBBIE ANN

Top Experience 📷

Learn Everything about Film at the Academy Museum of Motion Pictures

You'll be channeling your inner Tarantino at LA's multimillion-dollar film museum. Spectacular and expansive, it's a cutting-edge ode to motion arts and sciences, with thought-provoking exhibits, priceless memorabilia and a dynamic program of screenings and talks delving deep into celluloid culture. If you only have time for one museum in town, make it this one.

◉ MAP P96, D5

☎ 323-930-3000

www.academymuseum.org

cnr Wilshire Blvd & Fairfax Ave, Mid-City

🚌 Metro Lines 20, 217, 720, 780, DASH Fairfax Route

Exhibitions

Kick off with a visual overview of cinema's evolution in the Spielberg Family Gallery before tackling the core Stories of Cinema galleries on the second and third floors. These explore the many aspects of filmmaking, as well as showcasing movie memorabilia that includes Dorothy's ruby slippers from *The Wizard of Oz*. The East West Bank Gallery allows visitors to simulate the experience of walking onto Hollywood's Dolby Theatre stage to accept an Oscar, while the Marilyn and Jeffrey Katzenberg Gallery hosts large-scale temporary exhibitions.

Special Programs

The museum's 1000-seat David Geffen Theater and 288-seat Ted Mann Theater host year-round film screenings and discussions linked to various programs: 'Impact/Reflection' explores the sociopolitical aspect of cinema, 'In Conversation' features film artists in dialogue with personally inspiring figures, 'Inside the Academy' focuses on the history of the Academy and its eponymous awards, while 'Branch Selects' sees Academy members curating films significant to their specific craft. The museum also hosts weekend matinees.

Contrasting Architecture

Designed by Pritzker Prize–winning Italian architect Renzo Piano, the Academy Museum occupies two sharply contrasting buildings. Entry is via the restored Saban Building, a 1939, streamline moderne veteran that once housed a branch of the May Company department store chain. Directly behind it is Piano's new addition, a commanding, space-age sphere featuring a dome with 1500 glass panels. The dome crowns the Dolby Family Terrace, which offers arresting views of the Hollywood Hills.

★ Top Tips

○ Download the museum's free smartphone app, which offers added insight to enhance your experience of the galleries.

○ Check the museum website for upcoming screenings, which include family-friendly features and animation.

✕ Take a Break

While the museum is home to a cafe-restaurant, you'll find a greater range of options at the historic Original Farmers Market (p99) and adjoining Grove (p103) outdoor mall, located half a mile north on Fairfax Ave.

Top Experience 📷
Take in the Wealth of Art at LACMA

The depth and wealth of the collection at the largest museum in the western US is stunning. the Los Angeles County Museum of Art (LAC-MA) holds all the major players – Rembrandt, Cézanne, Magritte, Mary Cassatt, Ansel Adams – plus millennia worth of Chinese, Japanese, pre-Columbian and ancient Greek, Roman and Egyptian sculpture.

◎ MAP P96, D5

www.lacma.org

5905 Wilshire Blvd, Mid-City

adult/child $25/free, 2nd Tue of month free

🕐 11am-5pm Mon, Tue & Thu, to 8pm Fri, 10am-7pm Sat & Sun

🚌 Metro Lines 20, 217, 720, 780, DASH Fairfax Route

Rotating Exhibits

Construction of LACMA's ambitious expansion has limited the number of galleries currently open to the public. Despite this temporary shrinking, the museum continues to serve up an engaging, eclectic mix of exhibitions, with recent offerings including a retrospective on the work and legacy of 16th-century Chinese painter Qiu Ying and the country's largest-ever show dedicated to Fijian art. Permanent collection highlights include Chris Burden's outdoor installation *Urban Light* (a surreal selfie backdrop of hundreds of vintage LA street-lamps) and Michael Heizer's *Levitated Mass*, a surprisingly inspirational 340-ton boulder perched over a walkway.

Japanese Art Pavilion

LACMA's renovated, Zen-like Japanese Art Pavilion houses pieces ranging in origin from 3000 BCE to the 21st century. These include Buddhist and Shinto sculpture, ancient ceramics and lacquerware, textiles and armor, and the epic Kasamatsu Shiro woodblock print *Cherry Blossoms at Toshogu Shrine*. The pavilion itself is the work of the late American architect Bruce Goff, known for his organic designs.

Swiss Vision

Demolition of LACMA's mid-century pavilions began in 2020, making way for the bold vision of Swiss architect Peter Zumthor. His planned LACMA makeover will see the addition of airy, cantilevered galleries straddling Wilshire Blvd. The low-rise addition will make the most of LA's natural beauty, with floor-to-ceiling windows designed to show off the city, its hills and its celebrated natural light. Zumthor's redesign is scheduled for completion in 2024. Check the website for construction updates.

★ **Top Tip**

Short on cash? Visit on the second Tuesday of the month and you can have access to all collections and exhibits for free.

✗ **Take a Break**

Once you pay the relatively steep admission, odds are you won't want to stray too far from campus when your stomach grumbles. Just step over to **Ray's** (☎323-857-6180; www.raysandstarkbar.com; 5905 Wilshire Blvd, Los Angeles County Museum of Art; mains $18-37; ⏱11:30am-6pm Mon, Tue & Thu, to 9pm Fri, 10am-8pm Sat & Sun; 🅿🛜) for New American cuisine, or find a cheap and cheerful food truck across the street.

For reviews see

Melrose Ave

N Sweetzer Ave

N La Jolla Ave

N Crescent Heights Blvd

N Laurel Ave

N Edinburgh Ave

N Hayworth Ave

N Fairfax Ave

N Genesee Ave

Clinton St

Rosewood Ave

BEVERLY
CENTER
DISTRICT

Oakwood Ave

Beverly Blvd

W 1st St

S Edinburgh Ave

S Hayworth Ave

CBS Television
City

Farmers'
Market Pl

W 3rd St

Colgate Ave

S Orlando Ave

S Sweetzer Ave

S La Jolla Ave

S Crescent Heights Blvd

S Fairfax Ave

Gilmour La

MID-CITY

Los Angeles
County
Museum
of Art
(LACMA)

Wilshire Blvd

S Corning St

S La Cienega Blvd

N La Cienega Blvd

Academy
Museum of
Motion
Pictures

Wilshire Blvd

S San Vicente Blvd

La Cienega
Park

Petersen
Automotive
Museum

S Orange Grove Ave

S Ogden Dr

Alandele Ave

W Olympic Blvd

Miracle Mile & Mid-City

E

16 Melrose Ave

F

0   0   1 km
0   0.5 miles
☆14

G

MELROSE/
LA BREA
Clinton St

N Larchmont Blvd
(1.2km) →

H

1

2

N Spaulding Ave
N Stanley Ave
N Curson Ave
N Sierra Bonita Ave
N Gardner St
N Vista St
N Martel Ave
N Fuller Ave
N Poinsettia Pl
N Alta Vista Blvd
N Formosa Ave
N Detroit St
N La Brea Ave

Oakwood Ave

N Sycamore Ave

N Highland Ave

**FAIRFAX
DISTRICT**

15
☆

Beverly Blvd

**HANCOCK
PARK**

P

The Grove Dr

Pan Pacific Park

MID-CITY

S Gardner St
S Vista St
S Martel Ave
S Fuller Ave
S Poinsettia Pl
S Alta Vista Blvd
S Formosa Ave

W 1st St

S Orange Dr
S Mansfield Ave
S Citrus Ave
N Highland Ave
N Mc Cadden Pl

W 2nd St

3

W 3rd St

4

S Alta Vista Blvd

S La Brea Ave

W 4th St
S Sycamore Ave

S McCadden Pl

W 6th St

**MIRACLE
MILE**

W 6th St

5

2 ☉ La Brea
Tar Pits
& Museum

13 ☆

Wilshire Blvd

3 ☉ Craft
Contemporary

S Stanley Ave
S Curson Ave
S Ridgeley Dr
S Dunsmuir Ave
S Cochran Ave
S Cloverdale St
S Detroit St
S Orange Dr
S Mansfield Ave
S Citrus Ave

6

E   F   G   H

Sights

Petersen Automotive Museum

MUSEUM

1 MAP P96, D5

A four-story ode to the auto, this is a treat even for those who can't tell a piston from a carburetor. A head-lights-to-brake-lights futuristic makeover (by Kohn Pederson Fox) in 2015 saw the museum swag the prestigious American Architecture Award for significant new buildings. While we love its skin of undulating bands of stainless steel on a hot-rod-red background, it's what's inside that counts: four gripping, themed floors exploring the history, industry and artistry of motorized transportation. (☎323-930-2277; www.petersen.org; 6060

Wilshire Blvd, Mid-City; adult/senior & student/child $16/14/11; ◷10am-5pm Mon-Fri, to 6pm Sat & Sun; P ♿; 🚍Metro Lines 20, 217, 720, 780, DASH Fairfax Route)

La Brea Tar Pits & Museum

MUSEUM

2 MAP P96, E5

Mammoths, saber-toothed cats and dire wolves roamed LA's savanna in prehistoric times. We know this because of an archaeological trove of skulls and bones unearthed here, at one of the world's most fecund and famous fossil sites. Generations of young dino hunters have come to seek out fossils and learn about paleontology from docents and demonstrations in on-site labs at

La Brea Tar Pits & Museum

ALEX MILLAUER/SHUTTERSTOCK ©

the museum that now sits here. (☏ 213-763-3499; www.tarpits.org; 5801 Wilshire Blvd, Mid-City; adult/senior & student/child $15/12/7, every Tue in Sep & 1st Tue of month Oct-Jun free; ⊙ 9:30am-5pm; P ♿; ➤ Metro Line 20, DASH Fairfax Route)

Craft Contemporary   MUSEUM

3 ◉ MAP P96, E5

This intimate, well-respected museum showcases both world-renowned and local up-and-coming artists in the folk and craft art worlds. The museum's goal is to straddle the lines between the contemporary-art, sociopolitical movements and craft media you don't always see: fiber arts, metal working, book-binding and more. Hands-on workshops (several family-friendly) help pass along that knowledge. Exhibits change every few months, so check for details. (☏ 323-937-4230; www.cafam.org; 5814 Wilshire Blvd, Mid-City; adult/senior & student/under 10yr $9/7/free, by donation Sun; ⊙ 11am-5pm Tue-Fri, to 6pm Sat & Sun, 6:30-9:30pm first Thu of month; P ♿; ➤ Metro Line 20, DASH Fairfax Route)

CBS Television City   STUDIO

4 ◉ MAP P96, D3

North of the Farmers Market is CBS, where game shows, talk shows, soap operas and other programs are taped, often before a live audience, including the *Late Late Show with James Corden*, *Real Time with Bill Maher* and the perennially popular *Price is Right*

Hancock Park

There's nothing quite like the old-money mansions flanking the tree-lined streets of Hancock Park, a genteel neighborhood roughly bounded by Highland, Rossmore and Melrose Aves and Wilshire Blvd. In the 1920s, LA's leading families, including the Dohenys and Chandlers, hired famous architects to build their pads, and celebrities such as Damon Wayans, Melanie Griffith, Jason Alexander and Manny Pacquiao have lived here. It's a lovely area for a stroll or a drive, especially around Christmas when houses sparkle.

game show. Check online for tickets. (www.televisioncityla.com; 7800 Beverly Blvd; ➤ Metro Lines 217, 218, DASH Fairfax Route)

Eating

Original Farmers Market   MARKET $

5 ✕ MAP P96, D3

The Farmers Market is an atmospheric spot for a casual meal any time of day, especially if the kids are tagging along. Its narrow walkways are lined with choices: from gumbo and diner classics to tacos and pizza, sit-down or takeout. One of the better foodie options is cafeteria-style **Pampas Grill**

Larchmont Boulevard

Who dropped Mayberry in the middle of Los Angeles? With its stroller-friendly coffee shops, locally owned boutiques and low-key patios, Larchmont is an oasis of square normality bordering a desert of Hollywood hipness.

(☏323-931-1928; www.pampas-grill. com; Stall 618; combination platters per lb $12.65), a Brazilian *churrascaria* specializing in barbecued meats. (☏323-933-9211; www. farmersmarketla.com; 6333 W 3rd St; ⏱9am-9pm Mon-Fri, to 8pm Sat, 10am-7pm Sun; P🚼; 🚌Metro Lines 217, 218, DASH Fairfax Route)

Jon & Vinny's ITALIAN $$

6 MAP P96, D2

It might look like a Finnish sauna, but this oak-clad evergreen is all about simple, modern Italian cooked smashingly. Charred pizzas and the housemade pastas are the standouts, with soul-soothing meatballs also worth an encore. If it's breakfast, start right with olive-oil fried eggs with grilled kale, crispy potato, *'nduja* (spicy Calabrian paste) and preserved Meyer lemon. Reserve well ahead, especially for dinner. (☏323-334-3369; www.jonandvinnys.com; 412 N Fairfax Ave; breakfast $10-21, lunch & dinner pasta $15-24, mains $18-26; ⏱8am-10pm; 🚼; 🚌Metro Lines 217, 218, DASH Fairfax Route)

Republique CALIFORNIAN $$

7 MAP P96, G5

Republique sports several fetching hats: artisan bakery, light-filled cafe and buzzing bistro. Scattered with butcher-block communal tables, meat cabinet, marble bar and snug, woody backroom, its open kitchen pumps out daily-changing dishes made with prime produce. Translated, we're talking nourishing, globally inspired dishes like ricotta toast with citrus and pistachio, *sopes* with housemade chorizo or butternut-squash agnolotti with brown butter. (☏310-362-6115; www.republiquela.com; 624 S La Brea Ave, Mid-City; breakfast & lunch dishes $13-24, dinner mains $28-74; ⏱8am-3pm daily & 5:30-10pm Sun-Wed, to 11pm Thu-Sat; P📶🚼; 🚌Metro Lines 20, 212, 720)

Crossroads VEGAN $$

8 MAP P96, B1

Tal Ronnen didn't get to be a celebrity chef (Oprah, Ellen) by serving ordinary vegan fare. Instead, seasonal creations include 'crab cakes' made from hearts of palm, artichoke 'oysters,' and 'bechamel'-smothered eggplant, alongside pizzas and pastas incorporating innovative 'cheeses' made from nuts. Is that Jane Fonda? Tobey Maguire? Probably. The place is a hit with celebs; leave the Birkenstocks at home. (☏323-782-9245; www.crossroadskitchen. com; 8284 Melrose Ave, Mid-City; mains brunch $12-15, dinner $14-24; ⏱11am-2:30pm & 5-11:30pm Mon-Thu,

11am-2:30pm & 5pm-midnight Fri, 10am-2pm & 5pm-midnight Sat, 10am-2pm & 5-11:30pm Sun; **P** 🚗; 🚇Metro Line 10)

Canter's
DELI **$$**

9 🚇 MAP P96, D2

As old-school delis go, Canter's is hard to beat. A fixture in the traditionally Jewish Fairfax district since 1931, seen-it-all waitresses serve up the requisite pastrami, corned beef and matzo-ball soup, plus 24-hour breakfast, in a retro space deserving of its own '70s sitcom. (☏323-651-2030; www. cantersdeli.com; 419 N Fairfax Ave, Mid-City; mains $9-29; ⏰24hr; **P** 🚗 👶; 🚇Metro Lines 217, 218, DASH Fairfax Route)

Drinking

El Carmen
BAR

10 🚇 MAP P96, C3

Loud, dimly lit and festooned in bull heads and *lucha libre* (Mexican wrestling) memorabilia, this fun, well-stocked tequila tavern (over 300 to choose from) pulls an industry-heavy crowd. It's a big hit for weekday happy hour (5pm to 7pm) and a top spot to learn the difference between an *añejo* and a *reposado*. Alternatively, opt for a perfect tequila cocktail or an award-winning margarita. (☏323-852-1552; www.elcarmenla.com; 8138 W 3rd St, Mid-City; ⏰5pm-2am; 🚇Metro Lines 16, 17, 218)

Stark Bar
BAR

11 🚇 MAP P96, D5

The closest you can get to LACMA's *Urban Light* installation with a drink in hand, this bar on the museum's plaza pours draft cocktails, small-batch spirits and mostly Californian wines. Kick back with a Monterey chardonnay or a Oaxaca Meets Italy (mezcal, Campari, agave and lime) and graze on high-quality bites (including pizzas) from locavore Ray's (p95) next door. (5905 Wilshire Blvd, Los Angeles County Museum of Art; 📶; 🚇Metro Lines 20, 217, 720, 780, DASH Fairfax Route)

Paramount Coffee Project
CAFE

12 🚇 MAP P96, D2

Long, skinny spin-off of the Sydney original, this concrete-clad, plant-festooned hangout brings Aussie cafe culture to Fairfax. To the uninitiated, this means high-end specialty coffee and fresh, quality bites (dishes $6 to $20). Slurp a flat white while deciding between the coconut oats with housemade peanut butter, coconut yogurt and fruit, the radish-topped avocado toast or the egg, bacon and kale brioche roll. (☏323-746-5480; www. paramountcoffeeproject.com.au/ global; 456 N Fairfax Ave, Mid-City; ⏰7am-5pm Mon-Fri, 8am-5pm Sat & Sun; 👶; 🚇Metro Lines 217, 218, DASH Fairfax Route)

Entertainment

El Rey
LIVE MUSIC

13 ⭐ MAP P96, F5

Somewhat overlooked, this 1936 art deco dance hall is a brilliant live-music venue, with a killer sound system and excellent sight-lines. Best of all, while it can hold nearly 800 people, it feels a lot more intimate. Check the website for upcoming acts, which range from emerging singer-songwriters and rock outfits to some pretty big names. (www.theelrey.com; 5515 Wilshire Blvd, Mid-City; cover varies; 🚇Metro Line 20)

Groundlings
COMEDY

14 ⭐ MAP P96, F1

This improv school and company has launched no shortage of top talent, including Lisa Kudrow, Will Ferrell, Maya Rudolph and Melissa McCarthy. Its sketch comedy and improv can be belly-achingly funny, especially on Thursdays when the main company, alumni and surprise guests get to riff together in 'Cookin' with Gas.' (📞323-934-4747; www.groundlings.com; 7307 Melrose Ave, Mid-City; tickets $16-25; 🚇Metro Line 10)

New Beverly Cinema
CINEMA

15 ⭐ MAP P96, G2

Quentin Tarantino is the landlord at the New Bev, a vintage 1920s theater screening double features in 35mm. Check the website for the current schedule, a refreshing combo of black-and-white classics, modern (and obscure) cult hits and the odd vintage cartoon. Insomniac cinephiles take note: midnight screenings run on Friday and Saturday. (www.thenewbev.com; 7165 Beverly Blvd; ♿; 🚇Metro Lines 212, 312)

Shopping

Melrose Avenue
FASHION & ACCESSORIES

16 🔒 MAP P96, E1

This legendary, rock-and-roll shopping strip is as famous for its epic people-watching as for its consumer fruits. The strip between N Poinsietta Pl and N Fairfax Ave gets a lot of the buzz thanks to the boutiques stuck together like block-long hedgerows. Most of its gear is rather low-end, so if you're after the hipper, higher-end stuff, explore the long stretch between N Crescent Heights Blvd and N Almont Dr, or hit 3rd St. (🚇Metro Line 10)

Reformation
FASHION & ACCESSORIES

17 🔒 MAP P96, B1

Reformation is celebrated for its frocks, tops, jumpsuits, denim and more, pieces that meld style, simplicity and killer sass. Most pieces are part of limited-edition collections and all are designed and made right here in LA. Best of all, the brand prides itself on using sustainable and vintage fabrics and environmentally responsible production practices.

LNP IMAGES/SHUTTERSTOCK ©

Grove

Ecofriendly fashion *without* the granola. (📞213-459-6079; www.thereformation.com; 8253 Melrose Ave, Mid-City; 🕙11am-7pm Mon-Sat, to 6pm Sun; 🚇Metro Line 10, DASH Fairfax Route)

Grove

MALL

18 🔒 MAP P96, D3

Los Angeles' most famous alfresco mall pulls everyone from locals and tourists to the odd celebrity. Complete with fountain-studded piazza, vintage-style trolley and a movie-set feel, its retailers include higher-end department store Nordstrom, giant bookstore Barnes & Noble, Apple and a string of fashionable boutiques. It's also home to the mega doll emporium **American Girl Place** (www.americangirl.com) and celebrated Manhattan bakery Dominique Ansel. (📞323-900-8080; www.thegrovela.com; 189 The Grove Dr; 🕙10am-9pm Mon-Thu, to 10pm Fri & Sat, to 8pm Sun; 📶👪; 🚇Metro Lines 217, 218, DASH Fairfax Rte)

Walking Tour 🥾

Culver City Shuffle

Hollywood's milder-mannered sibling, Culver City has played a major role in the city's entertainment history, its studios churning out a string of movie and TV classics. Now also a burgeoning tech hub, it's one of LA's underrated pleasures, a liveable, vibrant neighborhood where Hollywood history meets polished hipness and cultural attractions, both innovative and quirky.

Walk Facts

Start Platform;
Ⓜ E Line to Culver City

End Helms Bakery District;
Ⓜ E Line to Culver City

Length 1.9 miles;
two hours

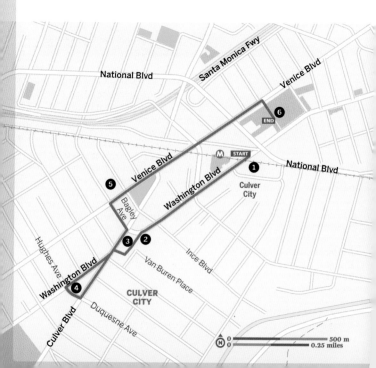

❶ Platform

Culver City's cool factor is exemplified by Platform, a buzzing, outdoor development harboring niche fashion and lifestyle stores, trendy coffee shops and tasty eateries. Stop by **Reformation** (www.thereformation.com; 8810 Washington Blvd; ⏰11am-7pm) for stylish, sustainable womenswear.

❷ Culver Studios

Many iconic movies were filmed at **Culver Studios** (9336 Washington Blvd; Ⓜ E Line to Culver City), including the original *A Star is Born*. Now home to Amazon Studios, its landmark Colonial-Revival mansion is featured in the opening credits of *Gone With the Wind,* also filmed on-site.

❸ Culver Hotel

A National Historic Landmark, the 1924 Culver Hotel is where 124 Munchkins slept three-to-a-bed while filming *The Wizard of Oz*. The 1939 movie classic was shot at the nearby MGM Studios, now known as Sony Pictures Studios.

❹ Kirk Douglas Theatre

A striking example of streamline moderne architecture, the **Kirk Douglas Theatre** (📞213-628-2772; www.centertheatregroup.org; 9820 Washington Blvd; 🚌Culver City Bus Line 1, Ⓜ E Line to Culver City) began life in 1946 as a movie palace. It has since been recast as an innovative playhouse, showcasing new works by local playwrights.

❺ Something Strange

Hidden behind an inconspicuous door, the **Museum of Jurassic Technology** (MJT; 📞310-836-6131; www.mjt.org; 9341 Venice Blvd; suggested donation adult/senior & student/under 13yr $10/8/free; ⏰2-8pm Thu, noon-6pm Fri-Sun; 👶; 🚇Metro Lines 33, 733, Ⓜ E Line to Culver City) is LA's most curious museum. It has nothing to do with dinosaurs and even less with technology. Instead, its labyrinth of curiosities includes a sculpture of the Pope squished into the eye of a needle. It may all be a mind-bending spoof, an elaborate hoax or a complete exercise in ironic near-hysteria by founder David Wilson.

❻ Roaming the District

Last stop is the historic Helms Bakery District, home to coveted furniture galleries and **Arcana** (📞310-458-1499; www.arcanabooks.com; 8818 Washington Blvd; ⏰11am-7pm Tue-Sun; Ⓜ E Line to Culver City). It is the city's best visual-arts book depot, with new, fine and out-of-print titles on its shelves and in its cabinets. If thirsty, slurp craft beers at **Father's Office** (📞310-736-2224; www.fathersoffice.com; 3229 Helms Ave; ⏰5-9pm Wed & Thu, 4-11pm Fri, noon-11pm Sat, to 9pm Sun; Ⓜ E Line to Culver City). If peckish, dig into fresh pasta at **Pasta Sisters** (📞424-603-4503; www.pastasisters.com; 3280 Helms Ave; pasta $10.50-18; ⏰11:30am-9:30pm Sun-Wed, to 10pm Thu-Sat; 🅿🛜🍴👶; Ⓜ E Line to Culver City).

Explore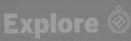

Santa Monica

Santa Monica is LA's cute, alluring, hippie-chic little sister, its karmic counterbalance and, to many, its salvation. Surrounded by LA on three sides and the Pacific on the fourth, in 'SaMo' boarders bob in the waves, real-life Lebowskis sip White Russians next to martini-swilling Hollywood producers, and celebrity chefs rub elbows with soccer moms at bountiful farmers markets.

The Short List

o **Palisades Park (p112)** Savoring sweeping bay views and glorious sunsets.

o **Santa Monica Pier (p108)** Riding the roller coaster, solar-powered Ferris wheel and antique carousel.

o **Third Street Promenade (p119)** Strolling this sunny pedestrian strip filled with boutiques and buskers.

o **Santa Monica Farmers Markets (p113)** Snaffling up LA's best produce, after all, this is where the chefs shop.

o **South Bay Bicycle Trail (p109)** Pedaling along the ocean for miles and miles.

Getting There & Around

Ⓜ The E Line (Expo) train takes about 50 minutes from DTLA.

🚌 Santa Monica's municipal Big Blue Bus travels around town and to the LAX Transit Center.

Neighborhood Map on p110

Palisades Park (p112) PGIAM/GETTY IMAGES ©

Top Experience 📷

Enjoy the Fun of the Fair at Santa Monica

No visit to LA is complete without at least a glimpse of this historic pier that features on just about every LA tourism ad. There are arcades, carnival games, a vintage carousel, a Ferris wheel, a roller coaster and an aquarium, plus snack stands, fancier restaurants and vendors selling crafts and souvenirs. Summertime brings a fun Twilight Concert Series (p118).

◉ MAP P110, A5

📞 310-458-8901

www.santamonicapier.org

Ⓜ E Line to Downtown Santa Monica

Pacific Park

Kids and kids within get their kicks on Santa Monica Pier at this small, classic Americana **amusement park** (📞310-260-8744; www.pacpark.com; per ride $5-10, all-day pass adult/child under 8yr $35/19; �-daily, seasonal hours vary; 👪), with a solar-powered Ferris wheel, tame roller coaster, family-friendly rides, midway games and food stands.

Santa Monica Pier Carousel

This charming **National Historic Landmark** (📞310-394-8042; Santa Monica Pier; adult/child $2/1; �-hours vary; 👪) at the beginning of the pier has 44 horses (and one rabbit and one goat), a calliope and a traditional soda fountain.

The Beach

There are endless ways to enjoy this 3.5-mile **stretch of sand** (www.smgov.net/portals/beach; 🚌Big Blue Bus 1), running from Venice Beach in the south to Will Rogers State Beach in the north. Sunbathing and swimming are obvious options, but you can also reserve time on a beach volleyball court, work out at the **Original Muscle Beach** (www.santamonica.com/original-muscle-beach-santa-monica; 1800 Ocean Front Walk; �-sunrise-sunset) or, for more cerebral pursuits, settle in at a first-come first-served chess table at **International Chess Park** (📞310-458-8450; www.smgov.net; 1652 Ocean Front Walk; �-sunrise-sunset), just south of the Santa Monica pier.

South Bay Bicycle Trail

The **South Bay Bicycle Trail** (�-sunrise-sunset; 👪) parallels the sand for most of the 22 miles between Will Rogers State Beach on the north end of Santa Monica and Torrance County Beach in the south. There are numerous bike rental shops along the beach.

★ Top Tips

o Admission to old-fashioned, low-key, family-friendly Pacific Park costs a fraction of Disneyland and Universal Studios Hollywood.

o The pier extends almost a quarter-mile over the Pacific. Stroll to the edge, and lose yourself contemplating the rolling, blue-green sea.

o Beachside parking fees can add up quickly. Take the Metro instead.

✕ Take a Break

Dogtown Coffee (www.dogtowncoffee.com; 2003 Main St; �-5:30am-5pm Mon-Fri, 6:30am-5pm Sat & Sun) is in the old Zephyr surf-shop headquarters, where skateboarding was invented during the 1970s. It brews great coffee and makes a mean breakfast burrito, preferred nutritional supplement of surfers the world over. Fun fact: Dogtown was the boarders' nickname for southern Santa Monica and Venice.

500 m
0.25 miles
0
0

F

20th St

16th St

15th St

21

E

26

Montana Ave

Idaho Ave

Washington Ave

California Ave

Wilshire Blvd

Arizona Ave

Santa Monica Blvd

19th St

18th St

17th St

16th St

15th St

14th St

Euclid St

12th St

11th St

10th St

9th St

Bay Cities

D

30

15 8

25

Lincoln Blvd

Lincoln Park

Lincoln Blvd

7th St

7th St

C

6th St

5th St

4th St

3rd St

2nd St

1st Ct

Ocean Ave

6th St

5th St

4th St

Arizona Ave

Third Street Promenade

18

27

24

Broadway

B

Annenberg
1 Community
Beach House

Alta Ave

Palisades Ave

Palisades Park

Palisades Park

19 17

20

2nd St

22 11

5

10

16

14

Santa Monica Place

Ocean Ave

Pacific Coast Hwy

Santa Monica
Information
Kiosk

A

Santa Monica
State Beach

1

2

3

4

Santa Monica

For reviews see

◉	Top Experiences	p108
⊙	Sights	p112
✕	Eating	p113
❊	Drinking	p117
✪	Entertainment	p118
⊞	Shopping	p118

Bergamot Station Arts Center (800m) ➎ ⑩

Memorial Park

Olympic Blvd ✕ 7

Santa Monica Fwy

Woodlawn Cemetery

Santa Monica College

16th St

14th St

Euclid St

Bay St

Pearl St

Pine St

11th St

Ocean Park Blvd

10th St

Lincoln Blvd

Lincoln Blvd

Colorado Ave

Pico Blvd

Pico Blvd

Santa Monica High School

6th St

4th St

Hollister Ave

✕ 9

Hill St

Ashland Ave

4th St

3rd Ave

Edgemar

⊙ 4

California Heritage Museum

28

29

⊙ 3

6 ✕

2nd St

Main St

✕ 13

Main St

Ocean Ave

✕ 12

Neilson Way

Bay St

South Bay Bicycle Trail

Barnard Way

✪ 23

Santa Monica Pier ◉

Santa Monica Bay

Santa Monica State Beach

Sights

Annenberg Community Beach House

BEACH

1 ⊙ MAP P110, A1

Like a fancy beach club for the rest of us, this sleek and attractive city-owned spot, built on actress Marion Davies' estate (she had a thing with William Randolph Hearst), opens to the public on a first-come-first-served basis. It has a lap pool, lounge chairs, yoga classes, beach volleyball, fitness room and art gallery. There's a cafe nearby, and it's set on a sweet stretch of Santa Monica Beach. (☎310-458-4904; www.annenbergbeachhouse.com; 415 Pacific Coast Hwy; per hour/day Nov-Mar $3/8, Apr-Oct $3/12, pool admission adult/senior/child $10/5/4)

Palisades Park

PARK

2 ⊙ MAP P110, B3

Perhaps it's appropriate that Route 66, America's most romanticized byway, ended at this gorgeous cliffside park perched dramatically on the edge of the continent. Stretching 1.5 miles north from the pier, this palm-dotted greenway sees a mix of joggers, tourists taking in the views, and resident homeless people. Sunsets are priceless. (☎800-544-5319; Ocean Ave btwn Colorado Ave & San Vicente Blvd; admission free; ⊙5am-midnight)

California Heritage Museum

MUSEUM

3 ⊙ MAP P110, B7

For a trip back in time, check out the latest exhibit at this museum

Santa Monica Farmers Markets

ANOUCHKA/GETTY IMAGES ©

housed in one of Santa Monica's few surviving grand Victorian mansions – this one built in 1894. Curators do a wonderful job presenting pottery, colorful tiles, Craftsman furniture, folk art, vintage surfboards and other fine collectibles in as dynamic a fashion as possible. (🕿 310-392-8537; www.californiaheritagemuseum.org; 2612 Main St; adult/senior & student/under 12yr $10/5/free; 🕘 11am-4pm Wed-Sun; 🅿; 🚌 Big Blue Bus Line 8, Metro Line 733)

Edgemar

NOTABLE BUILDING

4 ◎ MAP P110, B7

A shopping mall like no other, this was designed by Frank Gehry, whose signature LA work is the Walt Disney Concert Hall (p144). It's a relatively early design of his from the 1980s, but you'll see signature poured-in-place concrete, metal fencing and a soaring tower. Grab a coffee or ice cream at Blue Bottle or Ben & Jerry's and grab a seat to contemplate life by the fountain in the courtyard. (www.edgemar.com; 2415-2449 Main St)

Eating

Santa Monica Farmers Markets

MARKET $

5 🍴 MAP P110, B4

You haven't really experienced Santa Monica until you've explored one of its outdoor farmers markets stocked with organic fruits, vegetables, flowers, baked goods and freshly shucked oysters. The mack

Bergamot Station Arts Center

A former rail yard, **Bergamot Station** (off Map p110, F5; www.bergamotstation.com; 2525 Michigan Ave; 🕘 hours vary by business; 👪 🅿; 🚇 E Line to 17th St/Bergamot Station) has been converted to one of LA's best centers for galleries, mostly for contemporary art, alongside shops and a theater stage. Some 20 establishments keep varying hours, so check the website before setting out – or just wander. You're sure to find something to catch your eye.

daddy is the Wednesday market, around the intersection of 3rd and Arizona – it's the biggest and arguably the best for fresh produce, and is often patrolled by leading local chefs. (www.smgov.net/portals/farmersmarket; Arizona Ave, btwn 2nd & 3rd Sts; 🕘 8:30am-1:30pm Wed, 8am-1pm Sat; 👶)

Sunny Blue

JAPANESE $

6 🍴 MAP P110, B8

In Japan, *omusubi* (rice balls, aka *onigiri*) are an everyday staple, and this counter-service shop aims to make them popular Stateside. Before your eyes, the cheerful staff stuffs fluffy rice with dozens of fillings such as miso beef, spicy salmon and chicken curry – and veggie-friendly options like miso mushroom and hijiki seaweed – then wraps it in

Godmother of All Sandwiches

The signature sandwich at **Bay Cities** (Map p110, D4; 310-395-8279; www.baycities italiandeli.com; 1517 Lincoln Blvd; sandwiches $5.90-15; 9am-6pm Tue-Sun; P; M E Line to Downtown Santa Monica) – the best Italian deli in LA, period – is the sloppy, spicy Godmother (piled with salami, mortadella, coppacola, ham, prosciutto, provolone and pepper salad). It also has house-roasted tri-tip, eggplant parmigiana, tangy salads, imported meats, cheeses, breads and oils to salivate over. The outdoor seating is *meh,* so we take ours to the beach or Hollywood Bowl. Save time by ordering ahead.

a crunchy *nori* seaweed wrapper. (310-399-9030; www.sunnyblueinc. com; 2728 Main St; rice balls from $3.15; 11am-8pm Mon-Thu, to 9pm Fri & Sat, to 7pm Sun;)

Tacos Por Favor MEXICAN $

9 MAP P110, E5

This beloved counter-service hole-in-the-wall is dingy, hot and often crowded, with concrete floors, food served on paper plates and a menu so vast that you and your besties could eat breakfast, lunch and dinner here for a week and never order the same thing twice.

At least order *carne asada,* shrimp and chicken tacos and burritos. (310-392-5768; www.tacosporfavor. net; 1408 Olympic Blvd; tacos & burritos $4.25-14.95, combination plates $11-16; 8am-8pm; M E Line to 17th St/Santa Monica College)

Huckleberry CAFE $

8 MAP P110, D3

Part of the epicurean family from the couple behind Cassia (p116), Huckleberry's Zoe Nathan devises some of the most exquisite pastries in the city: salted caramel bars, crostatas bursting with blueberries, maple bacon biscuits, and pumpkin and ginger tea cakes. A simple fried-egg sandwich goes gourmet with Niman Ranch bacon, Gruyère, arugula and aioli. (310-451-2311; www.huckleberrycafe.com; 1014 Wilshire Blvd; mains $10-14; 8am-5pm)

Satdha THAI, VEGAN $

9 MAP P110, D7

This vegan Thai restaurant draws fans from all over town to an unassuming stretch of Lincoln Blvd for vibrant dishes such as endive cups filled with cashew 'tuna,' coconut, ginger, lemongrass, peanuts and more, green papaya or snap pea salads, beet-dyed noodles, and eggplant served catfish-style in curry paste. The vibe is comfy, contemporary and friendly. (310-450-6999; www.satdhakitchen. com; 2218 Lincoln Blvd; mains $10-14; 11am-3pm & 5-9:30pm Tue-Sun;)

Flower Child

CALIFORNIAN $

10 MAP P110, B4

Airy, fresh and fabulous, counter-service Flower Child is SaMo's go-to for contemporary, healthy, largely vegetarian salads, bowls, wraps and mains. The Mother Earth bowl brims with ancient grains, sweet potato, portobello mushroom, avocado and pistachio pesto, alongside sides like yuzu Brussels sprouts. Meat eaters can add proteins. Wash it all down with a serve-yourself assortment of iced teas. (310-382-2901; www.iamaflowerchild.com; 1322 2nd St; mains $9.75-16; ; M E Line to Downtown Santa Monica)

Uovo

ITALIAN, PASTA $$

11 MAP P110, B4

Some call this minimalist spot from the team behind Sugarfish (p116) 'fast-food pasta,' but if only other pasta places were this good. Noodles shipped directly from Bologna, Italy, are the mainstay (the magic is in the eggs). Queues may be long (no reservations accepted), but enjoy a glass of wine while waiting. (310-425-0064; www.uovo.la; 1320 2nd St; pastas $14-16; 11:30am-10pm; Metro 704, M E Line to Downtown Santa Monica, Big Blue Bus Lines 1, 2, 3, 5, 7, 8, 9, 18)

Stella Barra

PIZZA $$

12 MAP P110, B6

One of our favorite places on Main, it does a white pizza loaded with crispy kale, and another with prosciutto and egg on a bed of mozzarella and Gruyère. It makes its own pork sausage and the salads are tasty. Even the breakfast pizzas work. (310-396-9250; www.stellabarra.com; 2000 Main St; salads $13-15, pizzas $16-19; 5pm-midnight Mon-Thu, 11am-1am Fri, 10am-1am Sat, to 10pm Sun)

Library Alehouse

PUB FOOD $$

13 MAP P110, B8

Locals gather for the food as much as the beer at this wood-paneled gastropub with a cozy outdoor patio in the back. Angus burgers, fish tacos and hearty salads sate the 30-something, postwork regulars, while 29 handcrafted microbrews keep 'em hanging around till midnight. (310-314-4855; www.libraryalehouse.com; 2911 Main St; mains $16-23; 11:30am-midnight Mon-Fri, 11am-midnight Sat & Sun)

Ye Olde King's Head

BRITISH $$

14 MAP P110, B4

Fancy LA's best fish and chips? Or some bangers and mash, shepherd's pie or curry? This been-there-forever pub is a slice of 'jolly old' on the left coast. Breakfasts span beans on toast to the 'king size English breakfast' (eggs, bacon, sausage, beans, mushrooms, tomato – basically the full monty). (310-451-1402; www.yeoldekingshead.com; 116 Santa Monica Blvd; breakfast dishes $8-15, sandwiches & salads $12-17, mains $16-28; 9am-10pm Mon-Wed, to

11pm Thu & Fri, 8am-11pm Sat, to 10pm Sun; 🚌 Big Blue Bus Line 1, Ⓜ E Line to Downtown Santa Monica)

Santa Monica Seafood

SEAFOOD $$

15 🍴 MAP P110, D3

The best seafood market in Southern California offers a tasty oyster bar and sit-down market cafe, where you can sample delicious chowder, salmon burgers, albacore melts, oysters on the half shell and pan-roasted cod. It's been in business since 1939, but feels totally up-to-date. (📞 310-393-5244; www.santamonicaseafood.com; 1000 Wilshire Blvd; mains $14-28; ⏰ 9am-9pm Mon-Sat, to 8pm Sun; 🅿; 🚌 Big Blue Bus Line 2, Metro Line 20)

Sugarfish

SUSHI $$

16 🍴 MAP P110, B4

The Santa Monica shingle of a popular sushi chain imagined by LA's (reformed) Sushi Nazi, Chef Nozawa. You can order à la carte or one of the three set 'Trust Me' *omakase* menus, which are reasonably priced, filling and delicious. The special rice recipe offers just a hint of sweetness, and don't miss out on the blue crab roll. Phenomenal. (www.sugarfishsushi.com; 1345 2nd St; 'Trust Me' meals lunch $19-37, dinner $23-43; ⏰ 11:30am-10pm Mon-Sat, noon-9pm Sun; Ⓜ E Line to Downtown Santa Monica)

Fig

BISTRO $$$

17 🍴 MAP P110, B3

Set poolside at the Fairmont, and conceived with a coastal organic ethos, Fig sources many ingredients from the twice-weekly farmers market down the street. We love the 'bread balloon' with choice of spreads (hummus, eggplant salad etc) and the veggie-forward menu that's inflected with Middle Eastern tastes (lamb sausage pizza, wood-grilled fish with tahini). (📞 310-319-3111; www.figsantamonica.com; 101 Wilshire Blvd, Fairmont Miramar Hotel; mains lunch $14-29, dinner $26-64; ⏰ 7am-2pm & 5-10pm)

Cassia

SOUTHEAST ASIAN $$$

18 🍴 MAP P110, C4

Open, airy Cassia has made about every local and national 'best' list of LA restaurants. Chef Bryant Ng draws on his Chinese-Singaporean heritage in dishes such as *kaya* toast (with coconut jam, butter and a slow-cooked egg), 'sunbathing' prawns, and the encompassing Vietnamese pot-au-feu: short-rib stew, veggies, bone marrow and delectable accompaniments. Even the building is cool – the 1937 art deco Santa Monica Telephone Building. (📞 310-393-6699; www.cassiala.com; 1314 7th St; appetizers & sides $16-24, mains $37-39; ⏰ 5-10pm Sun-Thu, to 11pm Fri & Sat; 🅿)

Drinking

Bungalow
LOUNGE

19 MAP P110, B3

A Brent Bolthouse nightspot, the indoor-outdoor lounge at the Fairmont Miramar remains one of the hottest nights out in LA. Like most Westside spots, it can be too dude-centric late in the evening, but the setting is elegant, and there's still beautiful mischief to be found here. (www.thebungalowsm.com; 101 Wilshire Blvd, Fairmont Miramar Hotel; ⏱5pm-2am Mon-Fri, noon-2am Sat, to 10pm Sun)

Penthouse
ROOFTOP BAR

20 MAP P110, B3

On the top floor of the Huntley Hotel, the highest bar around Santa Monica Bay offers contempo-chic style and views from 18 floors up that may make you want to move here. It serves three squares plus a small-plates lounge menu, but don't miss the seasonal cocktails and signature concoctions like the Grapefruit Superstar and Thyme and Cucumber Amnesia. (☎310-394-5454; www.thehuntleyhotel.com/penthouse/nightlife; 1111 2nd St, Huntley Hotel; ⏱7am-11pm)

Bardonna
CAFE

21 MAP P110, E1

This neighborhood coffee shop is oh-so-LA. Think superfood coffee and tea drinks: matcha lattes, 'brain coffee' with MCT oil and ghee, sea-salt cold brew and CBD cappuccino. Breakfast and lunch foods span huevos rancheros, protein bowls and vegan donuts (mains $10 to $18). There's a handmade feel inside, or sit outdoors to watch the world go by on Montana Ave. (☎310-899-9500; www.bardonna.com; 601 Montana Ave; ⏱6am-7pm Mon-Fri, 7am-7pm Sat & Sun; 🚌Big Blue Bus Lines 18, 41, 42)

Onyx
ROOFTOP BAR

22 MAP P110, B4

Santa Monica's only indoor-outdoor roof bar has a swinging-'70s, Studio 54 vibe (brass-plated fireplace, hexagonal ceiling tiles), a bar made of a giant onyx slab (get it?) and cocktails such as the TamieTini (Ketel One, basil, passion fruit and cava) and the

Aero Theater (p118)

AKCLIPS/SHUTTERSTOCK ©

Shangri-La Mojito. But we most love surveying the view from the Pier to Malibu from seven stories up. (www.shangrila-hotel.com; 1301 Ocean Ave, Hotel Shangri-La; ⏱4pm-midnight Mon-Wed, to 2am Thu, 3pm-2am Fri & Sat, 3pm-midnight Sun)

Entertainment

Twilight
Concert Series
LIVE MUSIC

23 ✪ MAP P110, B5

This beloved local institution brings Santa Monicans of all stripes to rock out by the thousands on the pier and on the sand below, gigging local to world-famous names. (www.santamonica pier.org/twilight; admission free; ⏱Wed mid-Aug–mid-Sep)

Harvelle's
BLUES

24 ✪ MAP P110, C4

This dark blues grotto has been packing 'em in since 1931, but somehow still manages to feel like a well-kept secret. There are no big-name acts here, but the quality is usually high. Sunday's Toledo Show mixes soul, jazz and cabaret, and other nights might bring jam sessions or burlesque shows. (☎310-395-1676; www.harvelles.com; 1432 4th St; cover varies; Ⓜ E Line to Downtown Santa Monica)

Broad Stage
THEATER

25 ✪ MAP P110, D4

At the 499-seat, state-of-the-art Broad (rhymes with 'road'), the lineup of touring shows covers everything from new interpretations of classic Shakespeare to one-man productions, edgy plays and classical and world-music performances. It's the headline venue of Santa Monica College's performing arts complex; the main campus is about one mile southeast. (☎310-434-3200; www.thebroadstage.com; 1310 11th St; 🚌Big Blue Bus Lines 1, 8, 18)

Aero Theater
CINEMA

26 ✪ MAP P110, E1

Santa Monica's original movie theater (c 1940) is now operated by nonprofit American Cinematheque, where it screens old and neo classics, and offers Q&A sessions with bigwigs from time to time. Check its online calendar for upcoming shows. (www.american cinematheque.com; 1328 Montana Ave; 🚌Big Blue Bus Lines 18, 41, 42)

Shopping

Puzzle Zoo
GAMES

27 🔒 MAP P110, C4

Those searching galaxy-wide for the Lando Calrissian action figure, look no more. Puzzle Zoo stocks every imaginable *Star Wars* or anime figurine this side of Endor. There's also an encyclopedic selection of puzzles, board games and toys. (☎310-393-9201; www.puzzlezoo.com; 1411 Third St Promenade; ⏱10am-10pm Sun-Thu, to 11pm Fri & Sat; 🚼)

Jadis

GIFTS & SOUVENIRS

28 MAP P110, B8

Don't miss this homespun, steam-punk-paradise museum (entry $1) and shop, grinding with old gears and spare-part robots, antique clocks, concept planes and cars, old globes and lanterns – many of which were film props. Toys, games and other ephemera feature the same quirky aesthetic. (310-396-3477; www.jadisprops.com; 2701 Main St; noon-5pm Sat & Sun, phone to confirm)

Ten Women

ART

29 MAP P110, B8

This longstanding gallery sells art, folk art and crafts from a cooperative of 30 (it used to be 10) female artists. Always changing, but look for works in ceramic, wood, textiles, jewelry and more. (424-433-8116; www.tenwomengallery.com; 2719 Main St; 11am-7pm Mon-Thu, 10am-7pm Fri-Sun)

Great Labels

FASHION & ACCESSORIES

30 MAP P110, D3

Sensational secondhand couture and designer hand-me-downs from celebrity consigners. There's Oscar and Golden Globe gowns, elegant handbags, shoes and accessories from Pucci, Prada, Jimmy Choo and Dior. If you've ever wanted to pay $250 for a four-figure dress, come here. (310-451-2277; www.greatlabels.com; 1126 Wilshire Blvd; 10am-6pm Mon-Sat, 11am-5pm Sun)

SaMo Shopping

Covering three long blocks of downtown Santa Monica between Broadway and Wilshire Blvd, **Third Street Promenade** (Map p110, B4; 3rd St btwn Broadway & Wilshire Blvd; M E Line to Downtown Santa Monica) offers carefree, car-free strolling amid topiaries, fountains and street performers. **Santa Monica Place** (Map p110, B4; www.santamonicaplace.com; 395 Santa Monica Pl; 10am-9pm Mon-Sat, 11am-8pm Sun; M E Line to Downtown Santa Monica), just south of the Promenade, offers posh national and international chains. For more indie-minded boutiques, try high-end **Montana Ave**, north of downtown, and fun-and-funky **Main St**, heading south into Venice.

Explore ⬡
Venice

Come down to the Boardwalk and inhale a (not just) incense-scented whiff of Venice, a boho beach town and longtime haven for artists, new agers, road-weary tramps, freaks and free spirits. This is where Jim Morrison and the Doors lit their fire, Arnold Schwarzenegger pumped himself to stardom and Dennis Hopper once called home. These days, even as tech titans move in, the Old Venice spirit endures.

The Short List

o **Venice Boardwalk (p122)** *Witnessing street performers, fortune tellers, muscle men and bewildered tourists all having fun by the beach.*

o **Abbot Kinney Blvd (p127)** *Strolling and shopping America's coolest street.*

o **Venice Canals (p127)** *Admiring intimate homes around the waterways that lend Venice its name.*

o **High (p130)** *Sipping a seasonal cocktail and marvelling at the views from this rooftop lounge by the ocean.*

o **Venice Skatepark (p123)** *Watching skateboarders catch air – you may even feel airborne yourself.*

Getting There & Around

Ⓜ The E Line (Expo) is about 1.5 miles away, so ride hail.

🚌 Metro Lines 33 and 733, and Santa Monica's Big Blue Bus Lines 3 and 18. Line 3 connects to the LAX Transit Center.

Neighborhood Map on p124

Venice Skatepark (p123) JUST ANOTHER PHOTOGRAPHER/SHUTTERSTOCK ©

Top Experience 📷

Soak Up the Atmosphere on Venice Boardwalk

Prepare for a sensory overload on Venice's Boardwalk, a one-of-a-kind experience. Buff bodybuilders brush elbows with street performers and sellers of sunglasses, string bikinis, Mexican ponchos and cannabis, while cyclists and in-line skaters whiz by on the bike path, and skateboarders and graffiti artists get their own domains.

◉ MAP P126, A3

Ocean Front Walk

Venice Pier to Rose Ave

Murals

Venice Beach has long been associated with street art, and for decades there was a struggle between outlaw artists and law enforcement. Art won out and the tagged-up towers and the free-standing concrete wall of the **Venice Beach Art Walls** (www.veniceartwalls.com; 1800 Ocean Front Walk, Venice; ⏲10am-5pm Sat & Sun; 🚶), right on the beach, have been covered by graffiti artists from 1961 to the present.

Muscle Beach

Gym rats with an exhibitionist streak can get a tan and a workout at this famous **outdoor gym** (📞310-396-6764; www.laparks.org/venice/muscle-beach-venice-outdoor-gym; 1800 Ocean Front Walk, Venice; 1-/7-day pass $10/50; ⏲8am-6pm Oct-Apr, to 7pm May-Sep; 🚇Metro Line 733, 🚌Big Blue Bus Line 1) right on the Venice Boardwalk, where Arnold Schwarzenegger and Franco Columbu once bulked up.

Venice Skatepark

When Angelenos drained their swimming pools during a 1970s drought, board-toting teens from Venice and neighboring Santa Monica made their not-quite-welcome invasion and modern skateboarding culture was born. Well, as the bumper sticker says, 'skateboarding is not a crime,' at least not anymore, and if you needed further proof, this public, 17,000-sq-ft, ocean-view **skate park** (www.veniceskatepark.com; 1500 Ocean Front Walk, Venice; ⏲dawn-dusk; 🚇Metro Line 733, 🚌Big Blue Bus Line 1) is now a destination for both high flyers and gawking spectators. Look for great photo ops, especially as the sun sets.

★ Top Tips

o The Boardwalk is busiest on summer weekend afternoons, especially for the Sunday afternoon drum circle.

o Off-season, around sunset, crowds gather at cafes, bars and on the bike path.

o Late nights and early mornings are quietest – and also when you're most likely to encounter Venice's considerable homeless population.

✕ Take a Break

No place melds Old Venice and New Venice like the **Rose** (📞310-399-0711; www.rosecafevenice.com; 220 Rose Ave, Venice; brunch $10-20, mains lunch $14-30, dinner $17-45; ⏲7am-10pm Sun-Thu, to 11pm Fri & Sat; 🅿🚶). This airy institution dates from 1979 yet remains current, serving a diverse all-day menu to laptop-toting writers, tech geeks and Gold's Gym beefcakes.

Walking Tour 🚶

The Venice Stroll

Step into the Venice lifestyle and rub shoulders with folks who believe that certain truths will only be revealed to those who disco-skate in a Speedo-and-turban ensemble.

Walk Facts

Start Ocean Front Walk and Washington Blvd;
🚌 Culver City Bus Line 1

Finish Abbot Kinney Blvd;
🚌 Big Blue Bus Line 18

Length 3.5 miles; two hours

❶ South Venice Beach

Other piers along the coast have more action, but the beach around the Venice Pier is about as calm as it gets around these parts. The typical Venice crowds dissipate, golden sands unfurl, waves roll and beach volleyball games break out at a moment's notice.

❷ Venice Canals

From Washington Blvd, turn left at Dell Ave to reach this idyllic neighborhood that preserves 3 miles of waterways (p127) lined with eclectic homes, conceived by Venice's founder Abbot Kinney. Cross a few tiny drum-shaped bridges, and turn left at S Venice Blvd.

❸ Venice Boardwalk

The famed Venice Boardwalk (p122) is a vortex for the loony, the free-spirited, the hip and the athletic. Turn right down Ocean Front Walk.

❹ Muscle Beach

Ah-nold himself once pumped iron at this outdoor gym (p123) on the boardwalk. Now it's part workout space, part lookie-loo heaven.

❺ Venice Beach Art Walls

Make sure you have your camera at the tagged-up towers and concrete verticals of Venice Beach Art Walls (p123), open on weekends to aerosol artists.

❻ Venice Skatepark

This skatepark (p123) is an irresistible lure to skate punks and spectators, thanks to vert, tranny and street terrain with unbroken ocean views.

❼ Waterfront

At the indoor-outdoor beach bar **Waterfront** (www.thewaterfrontvenice.com; 205 Oceanfront Walk, Venice; ⏱10am-10pm Sun-Thu, to 1am Fri & Sat; 🚌Big Blue Bus Line 1, 🚈Metro Line 33), hipsters, surfers and shamblers rub elbows, quaffing beers, wines and Aussie-inspired coffees.

❽ Ballerina Clown & Binoculars Building

Where Rose Ave meets the beach, head inland to two Venice landmarks. Jonathan Borofsky's art piece *Ballerina Clown* levitates like a tweaked god/goddess above Main St. Diagonally across is the Binoculars Building (p128).

❾ Abbot Kinney Boulevard

From Main St, turn left onto Abbot Kinney Blvd (p127), the street brimming with chic boutiques and sensational restaurants. You won't need help window-shopping here.

✕ Take a Break

Put your feet up at one of the many cafes and restaurants along Abbot Kinney Blvd. For a quick bite, try the takeout counter at Gjelina (p130).

Venice

3rd Ave
4th St
Café Gratitude
17
Rose Ave
7th Ave
15
Binoculars Building 5
Gold's Gym 3
10
5th Ave
6th Ave
Sunset Ave
Vernon Ave
Pacific Ave
Main St
2nd St
Speedway
Ocean Front Walk
Indiana Ave
Brooks Ave
Plant Food + Wine
Homage to a Starry Night
Venice Beach
Broadway St
Abbot Kinney Blvd
Electric Ave
Westminster Ave
Venice Boardwalk
Westminster Ave
San Juan Ave
23
22
8
San Juan Ave
Abbot Kinney Boulevard
Santa Clara Ave
Venice Reconstituted
Market St
20
1
16
6
21
19
14
Linus (1km)
California Ave
Windward Ave
VENICE
13
7
12
Jim Morrison Mural
Venice Way
Grand Blvd
Dell Ave
Electric Ave
LA Louver
Mildred Ave
11
4
18
N Venice Blvd
Abbot Kinney Blvd
S Venice Blvd
Speedway
Santa Monica Bay
2 Canal Park
Venice Canals
Venice Canals
For reviews see
◉ Top Experiences p122
◎ Sights p127
✕ Eating p128
🄳 Drinking p130
🔒 Shopping p132
South Venice Beach
Dell Ave
9
Washington Blvd

Night + Market Sahm   THAI $

9  MAP P126, D6

The Venice outpost of chef-owner-Wunderkind Kris Yenbamroong's mini-empire specializes in take-no-prisoners spicy Thai dishes such as *nam khao tod* (crispy rice salad with soured pork, raw ginger and peanuts) and *larb gai* (spicy minced chicken), alongside standard-heat curry, noodle and veggie dishes. Pastrami *pad kee mao* is pure LA fusion: spicy 'drunken' noodles with pastrami from landmark Langer's Deli in Westlake. (☎310-301-0333; www.nightmarketsong.com/nm-sahm; 2533 Lincoln Blvd, Venice; mains $12-18; ⏰5-11pm Wed-Mon; 🚌Big Blue Bus Line 3, 🚇Metro Lines 33, 733, 🚌Culver City Bus Line 1)

Gjusta   CALIFORNIAN $$

10  MAP P126, C2

The folks behind the standard-setting Gjelina (p130) have opened this very casual, very gourmet, *very* Venice bakery, cafe and deli behind a nondescript storefront on a hidden side street. The menu changes regularly, but if we say lunches of chicken, cabbage and dumpling soup, and house-cured charcuterie and fish (such as gravlax, smoked Wagyu brisket and leg of lamb), does that help? Order at the counter, then go enjoy it all at a standing-room counter or on picnic tables in the backyard. (☎310-314-0320; www.gjusta.com; 320 Sunset Ave, Venice; mains $7.50-26; ⏰7am-9pm; 🚌Big Blue Bus Lines 1, 18)

Intelligentsia Coffeebar (p130)

MICHAEL GORDON/SHUTTERSTOCK ©

La Vida Vegan

Venice is LA's vegan capital. Most restaurants will have vegan options, but spots like **Plant Food + Wine** (Map p126, B3; 📞310-450-1009; www.matthewkenneycuisine.com/plant-food-wine-venice; 1009 Abbot Kinney Blvd, Venice; mains $14-26; ⏱noon-4pm Mon-Fri, 11am-4pm Sat & Sun & 5-11pm daily; 🍴; 🚌Big Blue Bus Lines 1, 18, Metro line 33) and **Café Gratitude** (Map p126, C1; 📞424-231-8000; www.cafegratitude.com; 512 Rose Ave, Venice; mains $15-18; ⏱8am-10pm; 🍴) set new standards with artfully presented vegan cooking.

Tasting Kitchen   ITALIAN $$$

11 ❌ MAP P126, D4

From the day-boat scallops in vermouth butter to the porcini-crusted hangar steak to the burger and the quail, it's all very good here. The pastas are especially delicious, as are the cocktails. Book ahead. (📞310-392-6644; www.thetastingkitchen.com; 1633 Abbot Kinney Blvd, Venice; mains $24-46; ⏱10:30am-2:30pm Sat & Sun & 5:30pm-midnight daily; 🚌Big Blue Bus Line 18)

Gjelina   AMERICAN $$

12 ❌ MAP P126, D4

If one restaurant defines the new Venice, it's this. Carve out a spot on the communal table between the hipsters and yuppies, or get your own slab of wood on the elegant stone terrace, and dine on imaginative small plates (raw yellowtail spiced with chili and mint and drenched in olive oil and blood orange) and sensational thin-crust, wood-fired pizza. (📞310-450-1429; www.gjelina.com; 1429 Abbot Kinney Blvd, Venice; mains $18-35; ⏱8am-midnight; 🚌Big Blue Bus Line 18)

Drinking

High   ROOFTOP BAR

13 🍸 MAP P126, B4

Venice's only rooftop bar is quite an experience, with 360-degree views from the shore to the Santa Monica Mountains – if you can take your eyes off the beautiful people. High serves creative seasonal cocktails (blood-orange julep, lemon apple hot toddy, Mexican hot chocolate with tequila) and dishes including beef or lamb sliders, meze plates and crab dip. Reservations recommended. (📞424-214-1062; www.highvenice.com; 1697 Pacific Ave, Hotel Erwin, Venice; ⏱3-10pm Mon-Thu, to midnight Fri, noon-midnight Sat, to 10pm Sun)

Intelligentsia Coffeebar   CAFE

14 ☕ MAP P126, C4

In this hip, industrial, minimalist monument to the coffee gods, perfectionist baristas – who roam the central bar and command more steaming machines than seems reasonable – never short you on foam or caffeine, and the Cake Monkey scones and muffins are addictive. The tunnel-like front vestibule is an oh-so-SoCal chill space. (310-399-1233; www.intelligentsia coffee.com; 1331 Abbot Kinney Blvd, Venice; 6am-8pm Mon-Thu, to 10pm Fri, 7am-10pm Sat, to 8pm Sun; ; Big Blue Bus Line 18)

Venice Ale House PUB

15 MAP P126, A1

A fun pub right on the Boardwalk on Venice's north end, blessed with ample patio seating for sunset people-watching, long boards suspended from the rafters, rock on the sound system and plenty of local brews on tap. Beer flights are served in a drilled-out skate deck, and the pub grub works. (www. venicealehouse.com; 2 Rose Ave, Venice; 10am-midnight Mon-Thu, to 2am Fri, 9am-2am Sat, to midnight Sun)

Townhouse & Delmonte Speakeasy BAR

16 MAP P126, B4

Upstairs is a cool, dark and perfectly dingy bar with pool tables, booths and good booze. Downstairs is the speakeasy, where DJs spin pop, funk and electronic music, comics take the mic, and jazz players set up and jam. It's a reliably good time almost any night. (www.townhousevenice.com; 52 Windward Ave, Venice; 5pm-2am Mon-Fri, noon-2am Sat & Sun)

Venice Beach Wines WINE BAR

17 MAP P126, C1

A sweet and cozy hideaway with louvered benches and tables so close together you will commune with strangers. Here, you may sip international wines by the glass or bottle (including a complex and invigorating French syrah) and munch charcuterie, *pizzettas* and the like. (310-606-2529; www.venicebeachwines.com; 529 Rose Ave, Venice; 4-11pm Mon-Thu, to midnight Fri, noon-midnight Sat, noon-11pm Sun)

Brig BAR

18 MAP P126, D5

Old-timers remember this place as a divey pool hall owned by ex-boxer Babe Brandelli (that's him and his wife on the mural outside). Now it's a bit sleeker and attracts a trendy mix of grown-up beach bums, arty professionals and professional artists. On **First Fridays** (www.abbotkinneyfirstfridays.com; 5-11pm 1st Fri of the month), the parking lot attracts a fleet of LA's famed food trucks. (www.thebrig. com; 1515 Abbot Kinney Blvd, Venice; 4pm-2am Mon-Wed, 2pm-2am Thu & Fri, noon-2am Sat & Sun)

Toms Flagship Store CAFE

19 MAP P126, C4

You know Toms, which made its name selling fun, slip-on canvas shoes and giving a pair away to underprivileged kids overseas for each pair sold in the States? Well,

JOE SCARNICI/GETTY IMAGES FOR TOMS/GETTY IMAGES ©

Toms Flagship Store (p131)

its flagship store doubles as a very chill cafe. Out back are a lawn, fireplace, shared tables and lounge seating in the sun and shade. A great hang. (📞310-314-9700; www. toms.com; 1344 Abbot Kinney Blvd, Venice; ⏰7am-9pm Mon-Sat, to 8pm Sun; 🛜🐾🚌Big Blue Bus Line 18)

Shopping

Aviator Nation   CLOTHING

20 🔒 MAP P126, C4

This beachwear brand's flagship and original store sells coastal-chic hoodies, tees and blankets, even guitar picks emblazoned with the signature stripes of yellow, orange and red. Behind the store is an awesome chill space with a

DJ station, ping-pong table and plenty of couches to chill and listen to the bands it sometimes brings in. (📞310-396-9100; www. aviatornation.com; 1224 Abbot Kinney Blvd, Venice; ⏰10am-6pm; 🚌Big Blue Bus Line 18)

MedMen   DISPENSARY

21 🔒 MAP P126, C4

Locals call MedMen the 'Apple store of cannabis.' Its shops' contemporary, minimalist design (Abbot Kinney is one of the largest) is so neat-as-a-pin one could just as easily imagine businessfolk in suits as stoners shopping for weed here. It's cannabis products are sold in many forms (smokable, vapable, edible, tinctures, mints) by friendly, knowledgeable staff in red T-shirts. (📞424-330-7232; www. medmen.com/stores/venice-beach-abbot-kinney; 1310 Abbot Kinney Blvd, Venice; ⏰10am-10pm; 🚌Big Blue Bus Line 18)

Burro   GIFTS & SOUVENIRS

This store (see 7 ❌ Map p126, D4), one of our favorite places on Abbot Kinney, deals in quality aroma-therapy candles, art books, a smattering of boho-chic attire for ladies, fair-trade beach bags from India and beaded jewelry. It serves tots at the kid's store two doors down. (www.burrogoods.com; 1409 Abbot Kinney Blvd, Venice; ⏰10am-7pm; 🚌Big Blue Bus Line 18)

A Brief History of Venice

In 1905, Abbot Kinney, a tobacco mogul by trade and a dreamer at heart, dug canals and turned fetid swampland into a cultural and recreational resort he dubbed the 'Venice of America.' For nearly two decades, crowds thronged to this 'Coney Island on the Pacific' to be poled around by imported gondoliers, walk among Renaissance-style arcaded buildings and listen to Benny Goodman tooting his horn in clubs. Most of the canals were filled and paved over in 1929 and Venice plunged into a steep decline until its cheap rents and mellow vibe drew first the beatniks and then the hippies in the '50s and '60s. These days, tech and entertainment dollars have fueled a hard-charging gentrification that is changing this once-low-key enclave yet again.

Strange Invisible

PERFUME

22 🔒 MAP P126, C3

Organic, intoxicating perfumes crafted from wild and natural ingredients, with names such as Aquarian Rose and Fair Verona, although some are gender neutral. Also sells dark chocolate. (☏310-314-1505; www.siperfumes.com; 1138 Abbot Kinney Blvd, Venice; ⏰noon-7pm Mon-Wed, 11am-7pm Thu-Sat, noon-6pm Sun; 🚌Big Blue Bus Line 18)

Salt

GIFTS & SOUVENIRS, ART

23 🔒 MAP P126, C3

Art, gifts and gifts that are art are the jam here. Artist-designed, one-of-a-kind trophies, snow globes with the F-word inside, handmade boxes that look like hardback books and ingenious children's books that even adults will enjoy. Whimsical, practical, fun and occasionally naughty. (☏310-452-1154; www.saltvenice.com; 1114 Abbot Kinney Blvd, Venice; ⏰noon-5pm Sun & Mon, 11am-6pm Tue-Sat, ; 🚌Big Blue Bus Line 18)

Walking Tour 🚶

Manhattan Beach, Beyond the Sand

A bastion of surf music and the birthplace of beach volleyball, Manhattan Beach has also gone chic. Its downtown area along Manhattan Beach Blvd has seen an explosion of trendy cafes, restaurants and boutiques. Yet, even with this Hollywood-ification, it remains a serene seaside enclave with prime surf on either side of the pier.

Getting There

🚗 Two exits off I-405 serve Manhattan Beach, including Rosecrans Blvd and Inglewood Ave, which merges with Manhattan Beach Blvd

🚌 Metro Line 109

❶ Sweat & Tumble

Sand Dune Park (www.citymb.info; cnr 33rd St & Bell Ave, Manhattan Beach; admission $3.16; ⊙by reservation from 8am daily, closing hours vary; 👪) requires reservations if you wish to access the long, deep 100ft-high natural sand dune for your requisite running/suffering.

❷ Uncle Bill's Pancake House

Tottering toddlers, sexy surfers and gabbing girlfriends – everyone comes to **Uncle Bill's** (☎310-545-5177; www.unclebills.net; 1305 N Highland Ave, Manhattan Beach; dishes $8-19; ⊙6am-3pm Mon-Fri, 7am-3pm Sat & Sun; 👪) for famous pancakes and big fat omelets.

❸ Photo Bomb

No surf, sport or music nut should miss the dazzling work on display at **Bo Bridges Gallery** (www.bobridgesgallery.com; 1108 Manhattan Ave, Manhattan Beach; ⊙11am-7pm, extended hours in summer). Bridges made his name photographing the likes of Kelly Slater at Pipeline.

❹ Indulge Your Ice Cream Addiction

There's a damn good reason hordes queue out the door of **Manhattan Beach Creamery** (☎310-372-1155; www.mbcreamery.com; 1120 Manhattan Ave, Manhattan Beach; desserts $4-8; ⊙10am-10pm Sun-Thu, to 11pm Fri & Sat). Its gourmet, housemade ice creams come served in a cup or cone or, better yet, a 'Cream'wich,' smashed between two freshly baked cookies.

❺ Hit the Beach

Ditch the shoes on the wide sweep of golden sand at **Manhattan Beach** (www.citymb.info; 🚉Metro Lines 126, 439). You'll find pick-up volleyball courts, a pier with breathtaking blue sea views, consistent sandy bottom surf and a giddy, pretty population that still can't believe they get to live here.

❻ MB Post

Trendy but friendly and unvarnished, **MB Post** (☎310-545-5405; www.eatmbpost.com; 1142 Manhattan Ave, Manhattan Beach; small plates $9-13, mains $11-39; ⊙5-10pm Mon-Thu, 11:30am-10:30pm Fri, 10am-10pm Sat & Sun; 👪) offers globally inspired cuisine. Walk in and dine at the long communal tables in the bar or reserve a more intimate table in the dining room. Attempt the Elvis dessert (chocolate pudding, peanut-butter mousse and bacon) if you dare.

❼ Ercoles 1101

A funky counterpoint to MB's design-heavy sports bars, **Ercoles** (☎310-372-1997; 1101 Manhattan Ave, Manhattan Beach; ⊙10am-2am) is a dark, chipped, cozy, well-irrigated hole with burgers to munch on and a barn door open to everyone from salty barflies to yuppie pub crawlers to volleyball stars.

Explore ⊕

Downtown

Take Manhattan, add a splash of Mexico City, a dash of Tokyo, shake and pour. Your drink: Downtown LA. Rapidly evolving, 'DTLA' is the city's most intriguing patch, where cutting-edge architecture and world-class modern-art museums contrast sharply against blaring mariachi tunes, Chinese grocers, abject poverty and many of the city's hottest restaurants, galleries, bars and boutiques.

The Short List

○ **Broad (p138)** *Musing on modern masterpieces at a cutting-edge art museum.*

○ **Walt Disney Concert Hall (p144)** *Catching a symphony in a Frank Gehry–designed showstopper.*

○ **Arts District (p146)** *Seeking out LA's coolest shops, eateries, bars and creative spaces, among them Hauser & Wirth.*

○ **Grand Central Market (p147)** *Sampling multiculti bites in a vibrant food market.*

○ **Rooftop bars (p151)** *Sipping Manhattan-style at rooftop bars like Perch.*

Getting There & Around

Ⓜ A/B/D/E Lines serve 7th St/Metro Center. B and D trains continue to Pershing Sq, Civic Center/Grand Park and Union Station. L Line trains reach Union Station, Little Tokyo/Arts District and Chinatown.

🚌 Metro buses connect Downtown to much of LA. DASH buses run five routes through Downtown. The LAX Flyaway shuttle departs from Union Station.

Neighborhood Map on p142

Grand Central Market (p147) LNP IMAGES/SHUTTERSTOCK ©

Top Experience

Marvel at the A-List Art at Broad

What do you do when you've got too much A-list art to handle? Build a cutting-edge museum, fill it with your blockbuster acquisitions and share it with the city. That's exactly what LA philanthropist and billionaire real-estate honcho Eli Broad and his wife Edythe did, with their 2000-strong collection considered one of the world's most prominent holdings of postwar and contemporary artworks.

◉ MAP P142, E2

☎ 213-232-6200

www.thebroad.org

221 S Grand Ave

admission free

🕓 11am-5pm Tue & Wed, to 8pm Thu & Fri, 10am-8pm Sat, to 6pm Sun

Ⓟ

Ⓜ B/D Lines to Civic Center/Grand Park

Collections

The first thing you should do at the Broad is register your name for a viewing of *Infinity Mirrors,* an extraordinary LED installation by Japanese artist Yayoi Kusama. Wait times can exceed an hour, though you're free to browse the museum until your viewing time, announced via text message. From the lobby floor, a 105ft escalator ascends through a space-grey cavity to the 3rd floor, where visitors are greeted by Jeff Koons' giant, stainless-steel tulips.

The surrounding galleries rotate works from the Broad's permanent collection, the strengths of which include classic 1960s pop art. Important works from this era include Robert Rauschenberg's JFK-themed *Untitled,* part of a series that saw Rauschenberg become the first American to win the Grand Prize at the Venice Biennale.

Architecture

The museum building is as much a talking piece as the collection within. Costing $140 million, the 120,000-sq-ft showpiece was designed by New York's Diller Scofidio + Renfro in collaboration with SF-based firm Gensler. It's 'shrouded' in a white lattice-like shell, complete with a 'dimple' (an oculus looking out onto Grand Ave) and corners that lift sharply at street level to let art lovers and the curious in and out.

Inside, the building bucks the museum tradition of hiding away its storage facilities. Here, 'The Vault' becomes an integral part of the design experience. Hovering between the 1st- and 3rd-floor galleries, it's pierced by the escalator connecting the gallery floors and visible through glass panels, offering visitors a voyeuristic peek at museum artworks lying dormant.

★ Top Tips

○ Reserve a timed museum ticket online; the line for same-day walk-ups can be long.

○ Viewings of Yayoi Kusama's *Infinity Mirrors* room installation can book out, so visit in the morning for your best shot of experiencing it. Check your phone regularly, as wait times are sometimes shorter than estimated.

○ Download the excellent Broad smartphone app, an audio guide offering insightful information on the art and artists. Museum docents are also knowledgeable and helpful.

✗ Take a Break

Refuel at the undercover Grand Central Market (p147), a buzzing foodie favorite located a 700yd walk away.

Walking Tour 🚶

Ghosts of Downtown

Downtown is the most historical and fascinating part of Los Angeles. Its streets are awash with the dreams of architects, designers and stars, translated into an extraordinary cache of buildings both breathtaking and whimsical. Thread your way through its multilayered streets to discover the treasures of Downtown's gilded past and its determinedly ambitious future.

Walk Facts

Start Eastern Columbia Building; Ⓜ B/D Lines to Pershing Sq

Finish US Bank Tower; Ⓜ B/D Lines to Pershing Sq

Length 1 mile; two hours

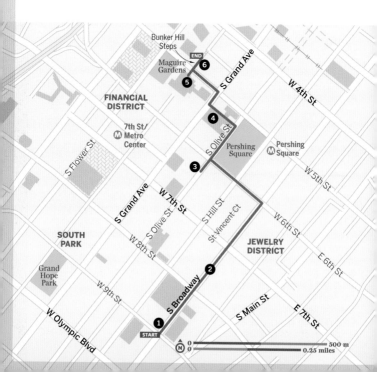

❶ Eastern Columbia Building

Rising at the corner of 9th St and Broadway, the 13-story Eastern Columbia Building is a masterpiece of art moderne architecture, clad in turquoise-and-gold terracotta tiles and featuring a gilded sunburst vestibule. Completed in 1930, it originally housed two clothing companies belonging to industrious Polish immigrant Adolph Sieroty.

❷ Broadway Theatre District

Spanning six blocks of S Broadway, the Broadway Theatre District once claimed the highest concentration of movie palaces in the world. At number 630, the **Palace Theatre** (☎213-629-2939; www.facebook.com/palace.theatre.la) is one of the oldest, dating from 1911. Across the street, the lavish **Los Angeles Theatre** (☎213-629-2939; www.losangelestheatre.com; 615 S Broadway) hosted the premiere of Charlie Chaplin's silent film *City Lights*.

❸ James Oviatt Building

From 1928 to 1967, Olive St's James Oviatt Building was home to fabled men's clothing store Alexander & Oviatt. Upon completion, the building's art deco lobby forecourt sparkled with 30-plus tons of glass by René Lalique. The French designer also designed the mailboxes, directories and the doors of the time-warped elevators.

❹ Millennium Biltmore Hotel

The Academy Awards were founded in 1927 at the grand Millennium Biltmore Hotel. The hotel's Historic Corridor features a fascinating photograph of the 1937 Oscars, held at the hotel once described as 'luxury heaped upon luxury' by the *Los Angeles Times*. The indoor pool is an art deco beauty (and the beds are supremely comfortable).

❺ Los Angeles Central Library

Designed by Bertram Grosvenor Goodhue, Downtown's **central library** (☎213-228-7000; www.lapl.org/branches/central-library; 630 W 5th St; ⏱10am-8pm Mon-Thu, 9:30am-5:30pm Fri & Sat, 1-5pm Sun; ♿) opened in 1926. Head straight for the second floor to gasp at its basilica-like rotunda, surrounded by the Technicolor, California-themed murals of Dean Cornwell.

❻ US Bank Tower

Destroyed by aliens in *Independence Day* and by a mega-quake in *San Andreas*, LA's tallest building to roof height makes for a commanding epilogue. Its **OUE Skyspace LA** (☎213-894-9000; www.oue-skyspace.com; 633 W 5th St, US Bank Tower, Downtown; adult/senior/child $28/25/22; ⏱10am-10pm, last entry 9pm; ♿) observation decks offer a spectacular 360-degree view of the city, hills, ocean and (in winter) snowcapped mountains.

A

23

Chick Hearn Ct

Grammy Museum 3

B Cottage Pl

Francisco St

C

D

Pasadena Fwy

1

S Figueroa St

W 12th St

S Flower St

7th St/Metro Center

ARCO Plaza

S Hope St

W 11th St

SOUTH PARK

Grand Hope Park

Macy's Plaza

W 7th St

Maguire Gardens

S Grand Ave

2

S Olive St

W Olympic Blvd

S Grand Ave

W 9th St

W 8th St

13 **FINANCIAL DISTRICT**

Midway Pl

S Hill St

21

JEWELRY DISTRICT

Pershing Square

S Broadway

24 Upstairs at the Ace Hotel

W 6th St

Pershing Square

Perch

22

S Main St

S Broadway

W 5th St

S Los Angeles St

California Market Center

S Spring St

15

26

3

Santee St

FASHION DISTRICT

S Main St

Harlem Pl

27

E 11th St

E 9th St

E 8th St

10

18

E 7th St

E 6th St

E 5th St

E 4th St

Maple Ave

Wall St

Flower Market

San Julian St

4

San Julian St

E Olympic Blvd

S San Pedro St

Winston St

Agatha St

Crocker St

Towne Ave

Stanford Ave

ARTS DISTRICT

5

E 7th St

For reviews see	
Top Experiences	p138
Sights	p144
Eating	p147
Drinking	p150
Entertainment	p152
Shopping	p152

S Central Ave

6

8

25

Warehouse St

11 19

B E 7th St

S Alameda St

A

B

C

D

E F G H

0 ——— 0.5 miles
0 ——— 1 km

Pasadena Fwy

1

W 3rd St

S Hope St

W 1st St

N Figueroa St

Santa Ana Fwy

W Cesar E Chavez Ave

Walt Disney Concert Hall

Mark Taper Forum

Broad ⊙ ⊙**1**

Ahmanson Theatre

N Grand Ave

Alpine St

2

⊙**2**

MOCA Grand

S Olive St

Civic Center/ Grand Park

Civic Center

W Temple St

Alpine Park

Yale St

Grand Central Market

Eggslut

Villa Moreliana

N Broadway

CHINATOWN

N Hill St

⊗**12**

N Broadway

3

N Spring St

Arcadia St

N Ord St

N Spring St

5

⊙ *City Hall*

N Main St

El Pueblo de Los Angeles Historical Monument

4

N Alameda St

N Los Angeles St

El Pueblo de Los Angeles

Discover Los Angeles Visitor Information Center

LITTLE TOKYO

E 3rd St

E 2nd St

Judge John Aiso St

Japanese Village Plaza

Imperial Western Beer Company

Union Station

Union Station/ Gateway Transit Center Ⓜ

Amtrak

4

James Irvine Garden

7 ⊙ *Japanese American National Museum*

Metrolink Station

N Vignes St

E Cesar E Chavez Ave

E 3rd St

14 ⊗

N Alameda St

E 1st St

E 2nd St

N Vignes St

Santa Ana Fwy

5

⊕ **20**

17

E 3rd St

S Garey St

6 ⊙ *Hauser & Wirth*

⊗ **9**

S Santa Fe Ave

6

E 4th St

⊕ **16**

E F G H

Sights

Walt Disney Concert Hall

NOTABLE BUILDING

1  MAP P142, E2

A molten blend of steel, music and psychedelic architecture, this iconic concert venue is the home base of the Los Angeles Philharmonic, but has also hosted contemporary bands such as Phoenix, and classic jazz musicians such as Sonny Rollins. The 2003 concert hall's visionary architect, Frank Gehry, pulled out all the stops for this building, a gravity-defying sculpture of heaving and billowing stainless steel. (☎323-850-2000; www.laphil.org; 111 S Grand Ave; admission free; ℗; Ⓜ B/D Lines to Civic Center/Grand Park)

MOCA Grand

MUSEUM

2 ◉ MAP P142, E2

MOCA's notable art collection focuses mainly on works created from the 1940s to the present. There's no shortage of luminaries, among them Mark Rothko, Dan Flavin, Joseph Cornell and David Hockney, in regular and special exhibits. Their creations are housed in a 1986 building by 2019 Pritzker Prize–winning Japanese architect Arata Isozaki. Galleries are below ground, yet sky-lit bright. Special exhibits usually cost $18. (Museum of Contemporary Art; ☎213-626-6222; www.moca.org; 250 S Grand Ave; admission free; ◷11am-6pm Mon, Wed & Fri, to 8pm Thu, to 5pm Sat & Sun; ♿; Ⓜ B/D Lines to Civic Center/Grand Park)

Union Station

KIT LEONG/SHUTTERSTOCK ©

Union Station

Built on the site of LA's original Chinatown, **Union Station** (Map p142, G4; www.unionstationla.com; 800 N Alameda St; P; MB/D/L Lines to Union Station) opened in 1939 as America's last grand rail station. It remains one of LA's architectural masterpieces, its Mission Revival style infused with both art deco and American-Indian accents.

The station even houses its own microbrewery, **Imperial Western Beer Company** (Map p142, G4; 213-270-0005; www.imperialwestern. com; 3pm-midnight Mon-Thu, to 2am Fri, noon-2am Sat, to midnight Sun; ; MB/D/L Lines to Union Station), occupying a cavernous annexe to the right of the main entrance. Until 1967, the annexe housed a branch of Fred Harvey House, a legendary restaurant chain famous for its straight-laced, all-female workforce. Known as 'The Harvey Girls,' they would inspire both Samuel Hopkins Adams' 1942 novel *The Harvey Girls* and MGM's 1946 musical spin-off, starring Judy Garland.

The LA Conservancy runs 2½-hour walking tours of Union Station on Saturdays at 10am (book online).

Grammy Museum

MUSEUM

3 MAP P142, B1

The highlight of **LA Live** (213-763-5483; www.lalive.com; P; MA/E Lines to Pico), this museum's interactive exhibits explore the evolution of the world's most famous music awards, as well as define, differentiate and link musical genres. Spanning three levels, its rotating treasures might include iconic threads from the wardrobes of Michael Jackson, Whitney Houston and Beyoncé, scribbled words from the hands of Count Basie and Taylor Swift, and instruments once used by world-renowned rock legends. (213-765-6800; www.grammymuseum.org; 800 W Olympic Blvd; adult/child $15/13; 10:30am-6:30pm Sun, Mon, Wed & Thu, 10am-8pm Fri & Sat; P; MA/E Lines to Pico)

El Pueblo de Los Ángeles Historical Monument

HISTORIC SITE

4 MAP P142, G3

A short stroll northwest of Union Station, this compact, colorful district is where LA's first colonists settled in 1781. Wander through narrow Olvera St's vibrant Mexican-themed stalls and check out the area's free museums, the best of which is **LA Plaza** (La Plaza de Cultura y Artes; 213-542-6200; www.lapca.org; 501 N Main St; admission free; noon-5pm Mon & Wed-Fri, 10am-5pm Sat & Sun;), offering snapshots of the Mexican-

American experience in Los Angeles. Free guided tours of the area leave from beside the **Old Plaza Firehouse** (☏213-485-8437; 134 Paseo de la Plaza; admission free; ⏱10am-3pm Tue-Sun); no reservations necessary. (☏213-485-6855; www.elpueblo.lacity.org; Olvera St; ⏱tours 10am, 11am & noon Tue-Sat; ♿; ⓂB/D/L Lines to Union Station)

City Hall
HISTORIC BUILDING

5 ◉ MAP P142, F3

Until 1966 no LA building stood taller than the 1928 City Hall, which appeared in the *Superman* TV series and 1953 sci-fi thriller *War of the Worlds*. On clear days you'll have views of the city, the mountains and several decades of Downtown growth from the observation deck. On the way up, stop off on level three to eye up City Hall's original main entrance, which features a breathtaking, Byzantine-inspired rotunda graced with marble flooring and a mosaic dome. (☏213-485-2121; www.lacity. org; 200 N Spring St; admission free; ⏱9am-5pm Mon-Fri; ♿; ⓂB/D Lines to Civic Center/Grand Park)

Hauser & Wirth
GALLERY

6 ◉ MAP P142, E5

The LA outpost of internationally acclaimed gallery Hauser & Wirth hosts museum-standard exhibits of modern and contemporary art. It's a huge space, occupying

116,000 sq ft of a converted flour mill complex in the Arts District. Past exhibits have showcased the work of luminaries such as Lucio Fontana, Louise Bourgeois and LA-based Larry Bell. The complex is also home to a standout art bookshop and gift store. The latter stocks a variety of gifts by local and international artisans, as well as collaborations with artists represented by the gallery. (☏213-943-1620; www.hauserwirthlosangeles. com; 901 E 3rd St; admission free; ⏱11am-6pm Tue-Sun; ⓂL Line to Little Tokyo/Arts District)

Japanese American National Museum
MUSEUM

7 ◉ MAP P142, F4

An informative (albeit expensive) first stop in Little Tokyo, this is the country's first museum dedicated to the Japanese immigrant experience. The 2nd floor is home to the permanent 'Common Ground' exhibition, which explores the evolution of Japanese-American culture since the late 19th century and offers a moving insight into the painful chapter of the US' WWII internment camps. Afterwards, relax in the tranquil garden and browse the well-stocked gift shop. (☏213-625-0414; www.janm. org; 100 N Central Ave; adult/senior & child $16/7, 5-8pm Thu & all day 3rd Thu of month free; ⏱11am-5pm Tue, Wed & Fri-Sun, noon-8pm Thu; ♿; ⓂL Line to Little Tokyo/Arts District)

Eating

M.Georgina

CALIFORNIAN $$$

8 ⊗ MAP P142, B6

San Francisco's Michelin-starred Melissa Perello is the talent behind this outstanding eatery-bar, part of the Row DTLA complex. Modern, Italo-influenced menus rotate around impeccable produce and the kitchen's wood-burning oven, translated into textured revelations such as semolina pasta with gorgonzola dolce, pickled treviso and candied walnuts and wood-baked black cod with creamed escarole. Also worth trying: the coal-baked potato, a surprising revelation. (📞213-334-4113; www.mgeorgina. com; 777 S Alameda St, B1 Suite 114, Row DTLA; mains $22-34; ⊙5-9pm Tue-Thu, to 10pm Fri & Sat, 3-9pm Sun; P🅿; 🚃Metro Lines 60, 62, 760)

Manuela

MODERN AMERICAN $$$

9 ⊗ MAP P142, E5

Part of the Hauser & Wirth arts complex, buzzing, loft-like Manuela remains a standout dining destination in DTLA. Staff are knowledgeable and happy to navigate you around an oft-tweaked menu that beautifully fuses local meats, seafood and produce with smoky Southern accents. The result is polished, attention-grabbing dishes like barbecued oysters with Calabrian-chili butter and wood-grilled sunchokes with cider-candied bacon and dill buttermilk. (📞323-849-0480; www. manuela-la.com; 907 E 3rd St, Arts District; mains lunch $16-32, dinner $22-49; ⊙11:30am-3:30pm Tue-Fri, 10am-3.30pm Sat & Sun & 5.30-10pm daily; 🐕; 🚃DASH Downtown A Route, Ⓜ L Line to Little Tokyo/Arts District)

Grand Central Market

Designed by Union Station architect John Parkinson, LA's beaux arts **Grand Central Market** (Map p142, E3; www.grandcentralmarket. com; 317 S Broadway; ⊙8am-10pm; 🐕; Ⓜ B/D Lines to Pershing Sq) is a neon-splashed bustle of counters peddling everything from artisan cheeses to oysters and *pupusas* (corn tortillas filled with cheese, beans, meat or vegetables). If you're undecided, opt for super-authentic *carnitas* (slow-cooked, Mexican-style pulled pork) tacos from **Villa Moreliana** (Map p142, E3; 📞213-725-0848; tacos $3.50, burritos $8; ⊙9am-6pm; 🧒) or pretty much anything from **Eggslut** (Map p142, E3; 📞213-625-0292; www.eggslut.com; sandwiches $7-9; ⊙8am-4pm; 🐕🧒). The latter is famed for 'the slut': a coddled egg nestled on top of potato puree poached in a glass jar and served with sliced baguette.

City Hall (p146)

Sonoratown

TACOS $

10 MAP P142, B3

One of LA's best cheap eats, this tiny, packed, critically acclaimed taqueria pumps out superb northern Mexican street food. The buttery tortillas – made in-house using lard and specialty Sonoran flour – are a worthy match for the succulent, mesquite-grilled meats. Choose from tacos, quesadillas and burritos, the latter also available in a smaller size so you can mix and match. Don't let any queue put you off; the wait is so, so worth it. (✆213-628-3710; www. sonoratown.com; 208 E 8th St; tacos $2.50, burritos $8.50; ⏰11am-10pm; ♿; ☐DASH Downtown E Route)

Bestia

ITALIAN $$$

11 MAP P142, C6

A boisterous, convivial Arts District 'it kid,' Bestia remains one of the most sought-after reservations in town; book at least a week ahead. The draw remains Chef Ori Menashe's clever, produce-driven take on Italian flavors, from charred pizzas topped with housemade 'nduja (spicy Calabrian paste) to rigatoni with sultry duck ragù, parmesan, star anise, pink peppercorn and dry seaweed. (✆213-514-5724; www.bestiala.com; 2121 7th Pl, Arts District; pizzas $19-21, pasta $21-32, mains $39-150; ⏰5-11pm Sun-Thu, to midnight Fri & Sat; ℗; ☐Metro Lines 18, 60, 62)

Howlin' Ray's

SOUTHERN US $

12 ✖ MAP P142, H3

It's hard to overstate the phenomenon that is noisy, takeout counter Howlin' Ray's. Customers gladly queue for two hours or more – check Twitter for current wait times. The reward: phenomenal, Nashville-style fried chicken, spiced from country (mild) to howlin' ('can't touch this!'). Get yours with bread and pickles in a 'sando' (sandwich) or try the weekend-only chicken and waffles. (📞213-935-8399; www.howlinrays. com; 727 N Broadway, Far East Plaza, Suite 128, Chinatown; mains $9-16; ⏱11am-7pm Tue-Fri, 10am-7pm Sat & Sun; 🅿; Ⓜ L Line to Chinatown)

V DTLA

INTERNATIONAL $$

13 ✖ MAP P142, C2

This jaw-dropping, jewel-like restaurant-bar-lounge occupies the historic Brock and Co. Jewelry store, once frequented by Hollywood royalty. Graced with stucco ceilings, contrasting street art, and a safe-turned-backroom, its polished, share-format offerings include next-level Genovese-style pizzas with combos like spicy salami, wild honey, mozzarella, red onions, chili, parmesan, rosemary and thyme. Cocktails are superb and a steal ($10 to $14) given the location. (📞510-858-6581; www.v.restaurant; 515 W 7th St; pizzas $14-18, share plates $11-18; ⏱4-11pm Sun-Wed, to late Thu-Sat; 🛜🍸; Ⓜ B/D Lines to 7th St/Metro Center)

Sushi Gen

SUSHI $$

14 ✖ MAP P142, E5

Come super early to grab a spot at this exceptional sushi spot, where Japanese chefs carve thick slabs of buttery *toro* (tuna belly), Japanese snapper and more. While the sushi counter serves superb à-la-carte options, your lunch goal is an actual table, where you can opt for the great-value sashimi lunch special ($19.50), which also includes miso soup, tofu and pickled vegetables. (📞213-617-0552; www.sushigen.org; 422 E 2nd St, Honda Plaza, Little Tokyo; sushi/sashimi combinations $15-35; ⏱11:15am-2pm & 5:30-9:45pm Tue-Fri, 5-9:45pm Sat; 🅿; 🚌DASH Downtown A Route, Ⓜ L Line to Little Tokyo/Arts District)

Gelateria Uli

ICE CREAM $

15 ✖ MAP P142, D3

Uli Nasibova's small-batch gelato is the bomb. Made with seasonal, locally sourced ingredients, flavors find their muse in LA's mish-mash of neighborhoods. Lick a San Gabriel Valley–inspired black sesame, a Filipinotown-channeling *ube* (purple yam) or Thai Town coconut-and-lemongrass. The silky consistency and sheer clarity of flavor is inimitable, which is probably why *LA Mag* proclaimed it the city's best. (📞213-537-0931; www.gelateriauli.com; 541 S Spring St; ice cream from $6.25; ⏱noon-10pm Mon-Wed, to 11pm Thu & Fri, 11am-11pm Sat, to 9pm Sun; 🍸♿; Ⓜ B/D Lines to Pershing Sq)

Drinking

Verve Coffee Roasters COFFEE

16 MAP P142, E6

Verve's Arts District flagship is suitably gorgeous: high timbered ceilings, plants, abundant natural light and a Southwest-inspired patio. Beans are roasted in-house, with specialty offerings including single-origin espresso and flash brew. The latter is one of several draft options, which might also include a honey-lavender draft latte and dry-hopped kombucha. You'll even find booze-free takes on libations like Old Fashioneds and Negronis. (213-419-5077; www.vervecoffee.com; 500 Mateo St, Arts District; 6:30am-8pm; DASH Downtown A Route)

Go Get Em Tiger COFFEE

17 MAP P142, E5

Surrounded by on-point boutiques and close to art gallery Hauser & Wirth (p146), light-washed, pretty-in-pastel Go Get Em Tiger pours superb specialty joe. Coffee options are rotated regularly, with two filter and two espresso options on standby. Specialty teas are available, along with a compact selection of quality grub, from cardamon shortbread to yeast-raised waffles with berries, ricotta and honey. (213-277-5558; www.gget.com; 827 E 3rd St, Arts District; 7am-6pm; DASH Downtown A Route, L Line to Little Tokyo/Arts District)

Varnish BAR

18 MAP P142, C3

Tucked into the back of the fabulously atmospheric **Cole's** (213-622-4090; www.pouringwithheart.com/coles; 118 E 6th St; sandwiches $9-16; 4pm-2am Mon-Thu, noon-2am Fri, 11am-2am Sat & Sun;) tavern is this dark, friendly, mixed-age speakeasy, an essential downtown bar since it won the Tales of the Cocktail competition in 2012. Perch at the bar or slip into a booth and trust the staff's impeccable suggestions. Live music (anything from funk to tiki) strikes up from around 9pm Sunday to Thursday. Cash only. (213-817-5321; www.pouringwithheart.com/the-varnish; 118 E 6th St; 7pm-2am; M B/D Lines to Pershing Sq)

Everson Royce Bar COCKTAIL BAR

19 MAP P142, C6

Don't be fooled by the unceremonious grey exterior. Behind that wall lies a hopping Arts District hangout, with a buzzy, bulb-strung outdoor patio. The barkeeps are some of the city's best, using craft liquor to concoct drinks such as the prickly-pear Mateo Street Margarita. Bar bites are equally scrumptious, with standouts including the buttermilk biscuits and roast-pork steamed buns. (213-335-6166; www.erbla.com; 1936 E 7th St, Arts District; 11:30am-2am Mon-Fri, 5pm-2am Sat, 2pm-midnight Sun; Metro Lines 18, 60, 62)

In Sheep's Clothing

COCKTAIL BAR

20 MAP P142, E5

Hidden inside Lupetti Pizzeria (it's through the door on your right as you enter), this Japanese-inspired listening bar sets a subdued, candlelit scene for quiet conversations over meticulously chosen turntable tunes. Discuss the virtues of hi-fi over craft sake, a sherry-cask rice whiskey or perhaps a Black Rose Mansion #2 (blended Japanese whiskey, vermouth and black walnut bitters). (213-415-1937; www.insheepsclothinghifi.com; 710 E 4th Pl, Arts District; noon-10pm Sun & Mon, to 1am Tue-Sat; DASH Downtown A Route, M L Line to Little Tokyo/Arts District)

Ham & Eggs Tavern

BAR

21 MAP P142, C2

Our favorite rock 'n' roll dive has it all: affable barkeeps, decent beer and vino, and a gritty, house-party vibe channeling Downtown pre-gentrification. It's tiny, dark and loud (especially later at night), serving up regular live rock and punk to a come-one, come-all crowd of fun-loving regulars. It's also easy enough to miss, masked behind the shopfront of a long-gone Chinese diner. (www.hamandeggstavern.com; 433 W 8th St; 5pm-1am Sun-Thu, to 2am Fri & Sat; M B/D Lines to 7th St/Metro Center)

Downtown Rooftop Toasts

Downtown makes the most of its taller-than-average buildings with a slew of buzzing rooftop bars. Top picks include fancy-pants **Perch** (Map p142, D2; 213-802-1770; www.perchla.com; 448 S Hill St; 4pm-1am Mon-Wed, to 2am Thu & Fri, 10am-2am Sat, to 1am Sun; ; M B/D Lines to Pershing Sq), a Gatsby-esque bar-restaurant crowning the Renaissance-Revival Pershing Square Building. Alternatively, head **Upstairs at the Ace Hotel** (Map p142, B2; www.acehotel.com/losangeles; 929 S Broadway; 11am-2am; ; M B/D Lines to Pershing Sq), a hipster hangout with a luxe, safari-inspired fit-out. Both offer $7 happy-hour cocktails on weekdays.

Precinct

GAY

22 MAP P142, D3

Climb the stairs to this sprawling, dimly lit, down-n-dirty, rock-and-roll-style bar where Downtown gays from twinks to bears frolic in a series of bars, dance floors and an indoor-outdoor area where smoking is permitted. Cover charge typically applies for Friday and Saturday club nights. (213-628-3112; www.precinctdtla.com; 357 S Broadway; 5pm-2am Mon-Fri, 3pm-2am Sat & Sun; M Lines B/D to Pershing Sq)

Entertainment

Staples Center
STADIUM

23 MAP P142, A1

South Park got its first jolt in 1999 with the opening of this saucer-shaped sports and entertainment arena. It's home court for the Los Angeles **Lakers** (☏888-929-7849; www.nba.com/lakers; tickets from around $80), **Clippers** (☏213-204-2900; www.nba.com/clippers; tickets from around $50) and Sparks basketball teams, and home ice for the LA Kings. The stadium also hosts pop and rock concerts. Parking costs $10 to $30, depending on the event. (☏888-929-7849; www.staplescenter.com; 1111 S Figueroa St; ♿; Ⓜ A/E Lines to Pico)

United Artists Theatre
LIVE PERFORMANCE

24 MAP P142, B2

A historic gem of a theater restored by the Ace Hotel, which curates the calendar. Offerings are eclectic, ranging from hip-hop, indie and spoken-word performances to internationally prolific comedy acts. Check the website for what's on. (Theatre at Ace Hotel; ☏213-235-9614; https://theatre.ace hotel.com; 929 S Broadway; 🚇Metro Lines 2, 4, 302, 745, Ⓜ B/D Lines to Pershing Sq)

Shopping

Row DTLA
SHOPPING CENTER

25 MAP P142, C6

Row DTLA has transformed a sprawling industrial site into a sharp edit of specialty retail and dining. It's like Tribeca, with better weather. Saunter pedestrianized streets for discerning apparel and accessories, designer homewares, niche fragrances, even Japanese bicycles. Top picks include stationery purveyor **Hightide Store DTLA** (☏213-935-8135; www. hightidestoredtla.shop; Garage Retail, Shop 140; ⏱11am-7pm Mon-Sat, to

---

Music Center of LA County

The **Music Center** (www.music center.org) is a touchstone of performing arts in America. **Center Theatre Group** produces works that have gone on to win Tony and Pulitzer Prizes. Venues include the **Walt Disney Concert Hall** (p144), the **Ahmanson Theatre** (Map p142, F2; ☏213-628-2772; www. centertheatregroup.org; 135 N Grand Ave; Ⓜ B/D to Civic Center/ Grand Park), which stages large-scale Broadway runs, and the intimate, theater-in-the-round **Mark Taper Forum** (Map p142, F2; ☏213-628-2772; www.centertheatregroup.org; 135 N Grand Ave; Ⓜ B/D Lines to Civic Centre/Grand Park). Showtimes vary by venue.

5pm Sun), affordable design store **Poketo** (☏213-372-5686; www.poketo.com; Shop 174; ⏰11am-5pm) and progressive unisex fashion label **Shades of Grey** (www.shadesofgreyclothing.com; Suite 110; ⏰noon-5pm Mon-Fri, 11am-6pm Sat & Sun). (☏213-988-8890; www.rowdtla.com; 1320 E 7th St; ⏰8am-10pm, individual shops & eateries vary; 🛜👫; 🚌Metro Lines 60, 62, 760)

Last Bookstore in Los Angeles

BOOKS

26 🔒 MAP P142, D3

What started as a one-person storefront is now California's largest new-and-used bookstore. And what a bookstore! Across two sprawling levels of an old bank building, you'll find everything from cabinets of rare books to an upstairs horror-and-crime book vault, book tunnel and smattering of art galleries. The store also houses a terrific vinyl collection and cool store-themed merch. (☏213-488-0599; www.lastbookstorela.com; 453 S Spring St; ⏰10am-10pm Sun-Thu, 10am-11pm Fri & Sat; 👫; Ⓜ️B/D Lines to Pershing Sq)

Last Bookstore in Los Angeles

Santee Alley

FASHION & ACCESSORIES

27 🔒 MAP P142, A3

Yes, it's an actual alley, open every day and packed with solid bargains spanning everything from denim, frocks, hoodies, shoes, baseball caps and tees to cell-phone covers, bling, eyewear, cosmetics and fragrances. (www.thesanteealley.com; cnr Santee & 12th Sts; ⏰9:30am-6pm; 👫; 🚌DASH Downtown E Route)

Top Experience 📷

Survey Three Great Museums at Exposition Park

A quick jaunt south of Downtown LA by Metro E Line or DASH bus, family-friendly 'Expo Park' began as an agricultural fairground in 1872 and has been a patch of public greenery since 1913. Today's draws here are a trio of great museums and the Los Angeles Memorial Coliseum, which has hosted two Olympics and is home to the USC Trojans (American) football team.

700 Exposition Park Dr, Exposition Park

P ♿

Ⓜ Metro's E Line runs from Downtown LA (10 minutes)

🚗 Take the Vermont Ave exit off the I-10 Fwy

California Science Center

Top billing at the **Science Center** (📞film schedule 213-744-2019, info 323-724-3623; www.california sciencecenter.org; 700 Exposition Park Dr; IMAX movie adult/senior & student/child $8.95/7.95/6.75; ⏰10am-5pm; 🚹) goes to the Space Shuttle *Endeavour,* one of only four space shuttles nationwide. There's plenty else to see at this multistory, multimedia museum dedicated to space, the human body, ecosystems and more.

Natural History Museum

From dinos to diamonds, this **museum** (📞213-763-3466; www.nhm.org; 900 Exposition Blvd; adult/senior & student/child $15/12/7; ⏰9:30am-5pm; 🅿🚹) takes you around the world and through eons. The beautiful 1913 Spanish Renaissance–style building stood in for Columbia University in the first *Spider-Man* movie.

California African American Museum

CAAM (📞213-744-7432; www.caamuseum.org; 600 State Dr; admission free; ⏰10am-5pm Tue-Sat, 11am-5pm Sun; 🅿🚹) showcases African-American artists and the African-American experience, with a special focus on California and LA. Exhibits change a few times each year in galleries around a sunlit atrium.

Los Angeles Memorial Coliseum

Built in 1923, this grand **stadium** (pictured; 📞213-747-7111; www.lacoliseum.com; 3911 S Figueroa St; guided/self-guided tours $25/10; ⏰guided tours 10:30am & 1:30pm Wed-Sun, self-guided tours 10am-4pm Wed-Sun) hosted the 1932 and 1984 Summer Olympic Games. Informative guided tours dish the history and take you inside locker rooms, a press box, on the field and more.

★ Top Tips

○ Roam the Natural History Museum at night on First Fridays for a lineup of live music and DJs.

○ When butterfly and spider pavilions are up, buy advance tickets to ensure entry.

○ **Lucas Museum of Narrative Art**, founded by *Star Wars* creator George Lucas, is set to open in 2023, covering works from the Renaissance to new media.

✕ Take a Break

Five-minutes' walk under the freeway is fabulous food hall **Mercado La Paloma** (www.mercadolapaloma.com; 3655 S Grand Ave; ⏰vendor hours vary; 🅿). Stalls sell everything from Yucatan cuisine to ceviche.

Walking Tour 🥾

Old & New in Pasadena

One could argue that there is more blue-blood, meat-eating, robust Americana in Pasadena than in all other LA neighborhoods combined. Yet beneath the preppy old soul, historical perspective and art and architectural landmarks, there are growing Asian influences and a (slightly) counterculture undercurrent.

Getting There

Ⓜ Metro L Line light rail serves Pasadena and connects it to downtown

🚗 Take CA-110 from Downtown or CA-134 from Burbank

❶ Circle the Rose Bowl

The venerable, 1922 **Rose Bowl Stadium** (📞626-577-3100; www.rosebowlstadium.com; 1001 Rose Bowl Dr) seats up to 93,000 spectators and shines every New Year's when it hosts the Rose Bowl college football game. At other times the UCLA Bruins play their home games here. Nearby, Brookside Park is nice for hiking, cycling and picnicking.

❷ Tour the Gamble House

There's exquisite attention to detail at the **Gamble House** (📞bookstore 626-449-4178, info 626-793-3334, tickets 844-325-0812; https://gamblehouse.org; 4 Westmoreland Pl; tours adult/senior & student/child $15/12.50/free; ⏰tours 10:30am, 11am, 11:30am, noon & 1pm Tue, 11:40am-3pm Thu-Sat, noon-3pm Sun; 🅿️), a 1908 masterpiece of Craftsman architecture built by Charles and Henry Greene.

❸ Enjoy World-Class Art

Rodin's *The Thinker* is only an overture to the full symphony of art at the exquisite **Norton Simon Museum** (📞626-449-6840; www.nortonsimon.org; 411 W Colorado Blvd; adult/senior/student & child $15/12/free; ⏰noon-5pm Mon, Wed & Thu, 11am-8pm Fri & Sat, to 5pm Sun; 🅿️). User-friendly galleries teem with choice works by Rembrandt, Van Gogh, Renoir, Raphael, Botticelli and Picasso. Free admission available after 5pm on the first Friday of each month.

❹ Steampunk Scene

An amazing boutique with a steampunk vibe, **Gold Bug** (📞626-744-9963; www.goldbugpasadena.com; 34 E Union St; ⏰10am-5pm Mon, to 6pm Tue-Sat, noon-5pm Sun) features collections by 100 area artists: portraits of dogs in Victorian suits, a robotic, metallic Cheshire cat, vintage furnishings and a terrific art-book collection.

❺ Asian Arts

In a stately 1920s Chinese Imperial Palace Courtyard–style building, the **USC Pacific Asia Museum** (📞626-787-2680; https://pacificasiamuseum.usc.edu; 46 N Los Robles Ave; adult/senior & student/child $10/7/free, 5-8pm Thu free; ⏰11am-5pm Wed-Sun, to 8pm Thu; 🅿️👫; Ⓜ️L Line to Memorial Park) covers the likes of Kabuki theater prints, Chinese ceramics and textile treasures in temporary exhibitions.

❻ Dinner & a Show

Sample fine California cuisine at the art-deco-inspired **Bistro 45** (📞626-795-2478; www.bistro45.com; 45 S Mentor Ave; pizzas $18-24, mains $27-49; ⏰5-9pm Tue-Thu, to 10pm Fri & Sat, to 8:30pm Sun; 🅿️; 🚇Metro Lines 180, 780, Ⓜ️L Line to Lake), followed by theater at the historic **Pasadena Playhouse** (📞626-356-7529; www.pasadenaplayhouse.org; 39 S El Molino Ave) or comedy at the legendary **Ice House** (📞626-577-1894; www.icehousecomedy.com; 38 N Mentor Ave).

Explore ⊗
Burbank &
Universal City

Home to most of LA's major movie studios – including Warner Bros, Disney and Universal – the sprawling grid of suburbia known as 'the Valley' is where the real folk live, making it more laid-back and down to earth than other areas in the city. Some local gourmet experiences are also well worth the trip.

The Short List

○ **Universal Studios (p160)** *Braving dinosaurs, rocketing on roller-coasters and perusing wizarding supplies at this movie-studio theme park.*

○ **Warner Bros Studio Tour (p164)** *Discovering the fun and fascinating behind-the-scenes world of movie making.*

○ **Sushi Row (p166)** *Heading to Studio City's Ventura Blvd, where dozens of sushi bars compete to wow diners.*

Getting There & Around

Ⓜ The Metro B Line (Red) runs from Downtown LA and Hollywood to Universal City and the North Hollywood (NoHo) Stations.

🚌 For travel to Ventura Blvd, get off the Metro B Line at Universal City Station and take Metro bus 150.

Neighborhood Map on p162

Warner Bros Studio Tour (p164) NATALIA MACHEDA/SHUTTERSTOCK ©

Top Experience 📷
Go Behind the Scenes at Universal Studios

Although Universal is one of the world's oldest continuously operating movie studios (since 1912), it's best known for the theme park in and around the studio's back lot. Despite the ebbs and flows of showbiz, the park remains a draw for generations of visitors and locals alike, thanks to an entertaining, regularly updated mix of thrill rides, live-action shows and a tram tour.

◎ MAP P162, E5

📞 800-864-8377

www.universalstudios
hollywood.com

100 Universal City Plaza,
Universal City

1-/2-day from $109/149,
child under 3yr free

🕑 daily, hours vary

P 🚻

M B Line to Universal City

Wizarding World of Harry Potter

At Universal's biggest attraction (expect long queues), climb aboard the **Flight of the Hippogriff** roller coaster and the 3-D ride **Harry Potter and the Forbidden Journey**. Buy wizarding equipment and 'every-flavour' beans in the fantasy-themed shops then dig into a feast platter with frosty mugs of butterbeer at **Three Broomsticks** restaurant.

Other Top Universal Attractions

Elsewhere in the park, the revamped **Jurassic World** ride is a float back to dinosaur days before a terrifying tumble through a land of raptors and T-rexes. **Revenge of the Mummy** is a short (but thrilling) indoor roller-coaster romp through 'Imhotep's Tomb' that at one point has you going backwards and hits speeds of up to 45mph. A ride based on **The Simpsons** sends guests rocketing along with the Simpson family to experience a side of Springfield previously unexplored. The delightful **Despicable Me Minion Mayhem** is certain to get the kids smiling.

Universal CityWalk

Flashing video screens, oversized facades and garish color combos (think Blade Runner meets Willy Wonka) animate **Universal CityWalk** (818-622-4455; www.citywalkhollywood.com; 100 Universal City Dr, Universal City; 11am-9pm Mon-Thu, to 11pm Fri-Sun; ; M B Line to Universal City), the outdoor shopping concourse adjacent to Universal Studios. CityWalk's 65 shops, restaurants and entertainment venues offer a mix of mid- and lowbrow attractions, with low leading by a nose.

★ Top Tips

○ Budget a full day to see Universal, especially in summer.

○ To beat the crowds, get there before the gates open or invest in the Universal Express Pass (from $159) or the deluxe guided VIP Experience (from $349).

○ Buying tickets online usually yields discounts and coupons.

○ General parking costs from $28 per day. If you're arriving by Metro subway, a free shuttle connects the park and Universal City station.

✕ Take a Break

There are plenty of dining choices at Universal CityWalk or we suggest heading to Ventura Blvd's Sushi Row, where you can splurge or have sneaky-good, affordable Japanese cooking at Daichan (p165).

For reviews see

◉ Top Experiences	p160
◉ Sights	p164
✖ Eating	p165
🍷 Drinking	p166
⭐ Entertainment	p167
🔒 Shopping	p167

W Burbank Blvd

Clean Ave

Vineland Ave

North Hollywood Ⓜ

Chandler Blvd

NORTH HOLLYWOOD

North Hollywood Park

Weddington St

14 ✖ Dundas Dr

W Magnolia Blvd

Magnolia Blvd

Colfax Ave

Otsego St

3 ◉ Hartsook St

NoHo Arts District

Bakman Ave

Lankershim Blvd

Clean Ave

Addison St

Camarillo St

Riverside Dr

Ventura Fwy

Hollywood Fwy

Ventura Fwy

Riverside Dr

Tujunga Ave

Lankershim Blvd

Cahuenga Blvd

Aroma Coffee & Tea

Moorpark St

Hollywood Fwy

8 ✖ ✖ 7

Colfax Ave

9 ✖ 🍷 12

Ventura Blvd

Arch Dr

✖ 6

Ⓜ Universal City

10 ✖

13 ⭐

STUDIO CITY

Laurel Canyon Blvd

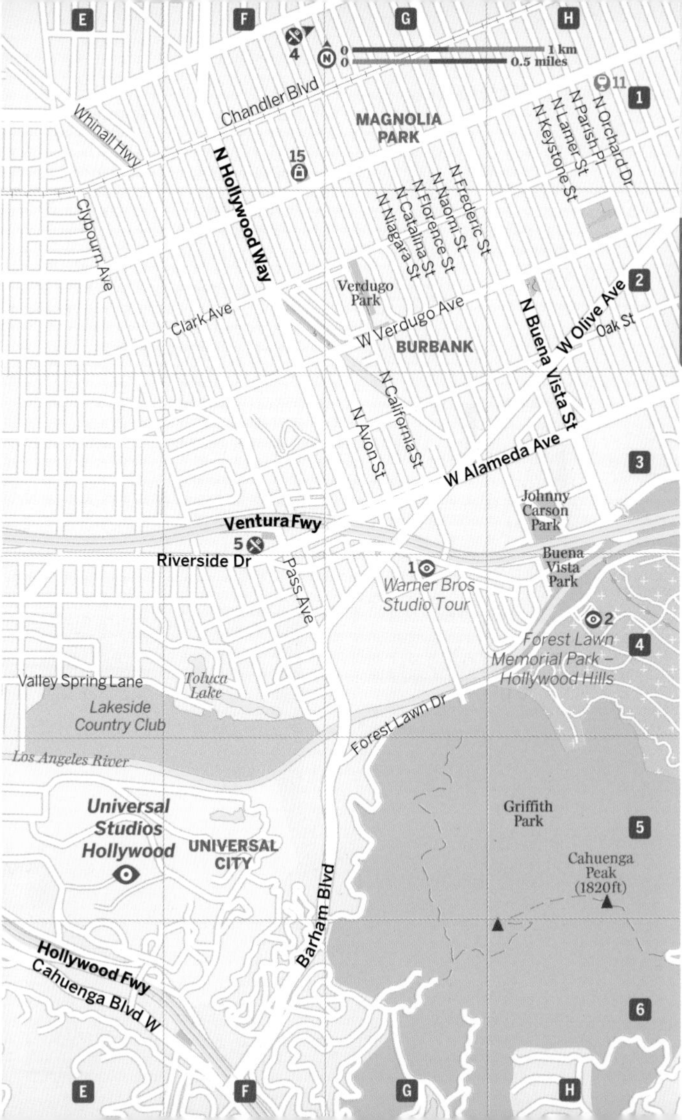

E F G H

Whinall Hwy

Chandler Blvd

MAGNOLIA PARK

N Orchard Dr
N Parish Pl
N Lamer St
N Keystone St

1

11

Clybourn Ave

N Hollywood Way

15

N Frederic St
N Naomi St
N Florence St
N Catalina St
N Niagara St

Verdugo Park

W Verdugo Ave

N Olive Ave

Oak St

2

Clark Ave

BURBANK

N Buena Vista St

N California St

N Avon St

W Alameda Ave

3

Johnny Carson Park

Buena Vista Park

Ventura Fwy

5

Riverside Dr

Pass Ave

1
Warner Bros Studio Tour

2
Forest Lawn Memorial Park – Hollywood Hills

4

Valley Spring Lane

Toluca Lake

Lakeside Country Club

Forest Lawn Dr

Los Angeles River

Universal Studios Hollywood

UNIVERSAL CITY

Barham Blvd

Griffith Park

5

Cahuenga Peak (1820ft)

Hollywood Fwy
Cahuenga Blvd W

6

E F G H

1 km
0.5 miles

Sights

Warner Bros Studio Tour   TOUR

1 ⊙ MAP P162, G4

This tour offers the most fun, yet authentic, look behind the scenes of a major movie studio. The two-hour standard tour kicks off with a video of WB's greatest film hits (*Rebel Without a Cause, Harry Potter* etc), before a tram whisks you around 110 acres of sound stages, back-lot sets including *Friends* and the *Big Bang Theory,* and technical departments, including props, costumes and the paint shop, and a collection of Batmobiles. More in-depth (and pricier) are tours themed for classic movies and a six-hour deluxe tour. (☏818-972-8687, 877-492-8687; www.wbstudio tour.com; 3400 Warner Blvd, Burbank; tours adult/child 8-12yr from $69/59; ⏱8:30am-3:30pm year round, extended hours Jun-Aug; 🚇Metro Lines 155, 222, 501 stop about 400yd from tour center)

Forest Lawn Memorial Park – Hollywood Hills   CEMETERY

2 ⊙ MAP P162, H4

Pathos, art and patriotism rule at this humongous cemetery next to Griffith Park. A fine catalog of old-time celebrities, including Lucille Ball, Bette Davis and Stan Laurel, rests within the manicured grounds strewn with paeans to early North American history. (www.forestlawn. com/parks/hollywood-hills; 6300 Forest Lawn Dr; ⏱8am-5pm; 🅿)

Bob's Big Boy

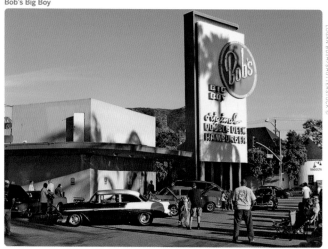

NoHo Arts District

NEIGHBORHOOD

3 ◉ MAP P162, C2

North Hollywood (NoHo) was a down-on-its-heels neighborhood of artists, but thanks to redevelopment it now boasts some 20 stage theaters in 1 sq mile and a burgeoning community of galleries, restaurants and vintage-clothing stores around them. (www.nohoartsdistrict.com; Ⓜ B Line to North Hollywood)

Eating

Chili John's

AMERICAN $

4 ✕ MAP P162, F1

Seen in *Once Upon a Time in Hollywood*, this neighborhood institution has been dishing out chili around a U-shaped counter since 1946. It's most popular served over spaghetti, but it'll also do chili dogs and sandwiches. Chili comes in beef, chicken and vegetarian versions, mild to hot. (☏ 818-846-3611; www.chilijohnsla.com; 2018 W Burbank Blvd, Burbank; mains $5-13; ⏱ 11am-7pm Mon-Fri, to 4pm Sat; Ⓟ 🚻; 🚇 Metro Line 145 to Keystone & Burbank Blvd)

Bob's Big Boy

DINER $

5 ✕ MAP P162, F3

Bob, that pompadoured kid in red-checkered pants, hasn't aged a lick since serving his first double-decker more than half a century ago. This Wayne McAllister–designed, Googie-style 1949 coffee shop is the oldest remaining location of this burger chain, serving a down-home menu centered around burgers, fries and chicken. (www.bigboy.com; 4211 W Riverside Dr, Burbank; mains $11.50-18; ⏱ 24hr; Ⓟ 🚻; 🚇 Metro line 155 to Riverside Dr & Rose St)

Daichan

JAPANESE $

6 ✕ MAP P162, C5

Tucked away in an unassuming mini-mall, and stuffed with knick-knacks, pasted with posters and staffed by a sunny, sweet owner-operator, this offbeat, home-style Japanese diner offers some of the best (and tastiest) deals on Sushi Row. Fried seaweed tofu *gyōza* (dumplings) are divine and so are the bowls – especially the *negitoro* bowl, which puts fatty tuna over rice, lettuce and seaweed. (☏ 818-980-8450; 11288 Ventura Blvd, Studio City; mains $8-20; ⏱ 11:30am-3pm & 5:30-9pm Mon-Fri, noon-3pm & 5-9pm Sat; Ⓟ)

Caioti Pizza Cafe

ITALIAN $$

7 ✕ MAP P162, C4

This long-loved Italian cafe serves salads, bison burgers and Italian sausage sandwiches, as well as some terrific pizzas and pastas. But it's the 'THE' Salad (romaine, watercress, walnuts and gorgonzola) that has become an urban legend; it's been known to induce labor in pregnant women. (www.caiotipizzacafe.com; 4346 Tujunga Ave, Studio City; mains $10-18; ⏱ 10am-10pm Mon-Thu, to 11pm Fri, 9am-11pm Sat, to 10:30pm Sun)

Aroma Coffee & Tea

This popular **cafe** (Map p162, C4; www.aromacoffeeandtea.com; 4360 Tujunga Ave, Studio City; mains $11-15; ⏰6am-11pm) is in a converted, artsy, multiroom (yet somehow still cozy) house; outside, tables crowd leafy, heated patios and the line runs out the door. Coffees are great and the humongous menu runs from breakfast enchiladas to salads to burgers.

Vitello's   ITALIAN $$

8 🍴 MAP P162, B4

This sophisticated spot with brick and black-mottled walls has been in business since 1964 thanks to Italian classics, burgers, steaks (the bone-in angus steak will set you back $46) and an entire plant-based menu. Upstairs, **Feinstein's at Vitello's** features Liza Minelli artwork, custom cocktails, and crooners of jazz and the great American songbook (cover varies). (📞818-769-0905; www.vitellos restaurant.com; 4349 Tujunga Ave, Studio City; mains $12-34; ⏰11am-10pm Mon-Thu, to 11pm Fri & Sat; P🍷)

Asanebo   SUSHI $$$

9 🍴 MAP P162, A4

Although it's in a strip mall (welcome to the Valley), Asanebo is a Sushi Row standout thanks to dishes such as halibut sashimi with fresh truffle and *kanpachi* (amberjack) with miso and serrano chilies. Chef Tetsuya Nakao has a Michelin star under his belt and helped launch chef Nobu Matsuhisa toward his Nobu Japanese restaurant empire. (📞818-760-3348; www.asanebo-restaurant.com; 11941 Ventura Blvd, Studio City; sushi $6-24; ⏰noon-2pm & 6-10:30pm Tue-Fri, 6-10:30pm Sat, 6-10pm Sun; P; 🚆Metro Lines 150, 240)

Kazu Sushi   JAPANESE $$$

10 🍴 MAP P162, B5

Stuck in a cramped and otherwise nondescript, split-level minimall that's easy to miss is one of the best-kept secrets among LA's sushi aficionados. Kazu Sushi is Michelin-rated, very high-end, has a terrific sake selection and is worth the splurge on the *omakase* (chef's choice) menu. (📞818-763-4836; www.kazusushi818.com; 11440 Ventura Blvd, Studio City; dishes $7.50-22, omakase from $60; ⏰noon-2pm & 6-9:45pm Mon-Fri, 6-9:45pm Sat; P)

Drinking

Tony's Darts Away   CRAFT BEER

11 🍺 MAP P162, H1

This old-shoe-comfy neighborhood bar is renowned for its extraordinary beer selection – a changing choice of 38 craft beers on tap, plus wines and ciders. The food menu features sausages ($8 to $10) along with burgers and snacks. Tony's does its part for the environment, too. Food is organically raised wherever possible, and all of the beers, wines, breads and meats come from California for a smaller environmental footprint. (☎818-253-1710; www.tonysda.com; 1710 W Magnolia Blvd, Burbank; ☺noon-2am Mon-Thu, 11am-2am Fri, 10am-2am Sat, 11am-1am Sun; 🚃Metro Line 183)

Black Market Liquor Bar   BAR

12 MAP P162, A5

Under a vaulted brick ceiling, this upscale neighborhood tavern had us at its list of Bloodys (Mary with vodka, Maria with tequila, hell with gin etc), make-your-own mimosas, unusual cocktails and offbeat beers flavored with watermelon, grapefruit and coffee. They go great with plates such as fried cauliflower with lemon aioli and meatballs with garlic crisps. (☎818-446-2533; www.blackmarket liquorbar.com; 11915 Ventura Blvd, Studio City; ☺5pm-1am Mon-Fri, 11am-3pm & 5pm-1am Sat & Sun)

Entertainment

Baked Potato   JAZZ, BLUES

13 ⭐ MAP P162, D5

Near Universal Studios, a dancing spud beckons you inside this diminutive jazz-and-blues hall – LA's oldest – where the schedule mixes no-names with big-timers. Drinks are stiff and vittles include (yep!) baked potatoes ($10 to $18) in 24 flavors. (www.thebakedpotato.com; 3787 Cahuenga Blvd, Studio City; cover $10-25, plus 2 drinks; ☺7pm-2am; Ⓜ B Line to Universal City)

El Portal   THEATER

14 ⭐ MAP P162, C2

The stage of this one-time vaudeville house from 1926 has been graced by headliners from Debbie Reynolds to James Corden. Restored to its former glory after the 1994 Northridge earthquake, it's now a mainstay of the NoHo Arts District. (www.elportaltheatre.com; 5269 Lankershim Blvd, North Hollywood; Ⓜ B Line to North Hollywood)

Shopping

It's a Wrap!   CLOTHING

15 🔒 MAP P162, F1

Darling, once TV and film stars wear clothing on screen, you don't seriously think it'll get another airing? That's where this shop comes in: reselling great garb from the latest shows. (www.itsawraphollywood.com; 3315 W Magnolia Blvd, Burbank; ☺11am-8pm Mon-Fri, to 6pm Sat & Sun)

Worth a Trip 🔭

Check Out the Beauty & Beautiful People at Malibu

Everyone needs a little Malibu. Here's a moneyed, stylish yet laid-back beach town and celebrity enclave that rambles for 27 miles along the Pacific Coast Hwy, blessed with the stunning natural beauty of its coastal mountains, pristine coves, wide sweeps of golden sand and epic waves.

🚗 The I-10 Fwy becomes California Hwy 1 north in Santa Monica.

🚌 Metro's Malibu Express Line 534 leaves from Fairfax Ave and Washington Blvd.

Getty Villa

Stunningly perched on an ocean-view hill-side, the replica 1st-century Roman **Getty Villa** (☏310-430-7300; www.getty.edu; 17985 Pacific Coast Hwy, Pacific Palisades; admission free; ⏰10am-5pm Wed-Mon; **P**⛴; 🚊Metro Line 534 to Coastline Dr) is an exquisite, 64-acre showcase for Greek, Roman and Etruscan antiquities, in galleries, courtyards, lush gardens and the brain-bending Hall of Colored Marbles.

Malibu Pier

The **pier** (www.malibupier.com; 23000 Pacific Coast Hwy, Malibu; parking rates vary by season; ⏰6:30am-sunset; **P**; 🚊Metro Line 534) marks the beginning of Malibu's commercial heart. It's open for strolling and license-free fishing and delivers fine views of surfers riding waves off Surfrider Beach.

El Matador State Beach

El Matador (pictured; ☏818-880-0363; www.parks.ca.gov; 32215 Pacific Coast Hwy, Malibu; **P**) is arguably Malibu's most stunning beach. Stroll down the bluffs to sandstone rock towers that rise from emerald coves. Sunbathers stroll through the tides and dolphins breech beyond the waves.

Nobu Malibu

An outpost of Chef Nobu Matsuhisa's empire of luxe Japanese restaurants, **Nobu Malibu** (☏310-317-9140; www.noburestaurants.com/malibu; 22706 Pacific Coast Hwy, Malibu; dishes $18-78; ⏰noon-10pm Mon-Thu, 9am-11pm Fri & Sat, to 10pm Sun; **P**; 🚊Metro Line 534) is consistently one of LA's hot spots, with a high celeb quotient. It's a cavernous, modern wood chalet with sushi bar, dining room and patio overlooking the swirling sea.

★ Top Tips

○ Unless you strike gold and find free parking on Pacific Coast Hwy, lot parking rates vary daily and seasonally ($6 to $15).

○ Malibu is best explored midweek; you'll have the roads and beaches mostly to yourself.

✕ Take a Break

Whitewashed dining rooms at **Malibu Farm** (☏310-456-1112; www.malibu-farm.com; 23000 Pacific Coast Hwy, Malibu Pier, Malibu; mains breakfast $14-20, lunch & dinner $17-38; ⏰7am-9pm Sun-Fri, to 10pm Sat; 🚊Metro Line 534) make for beachy keen munching on farm-to-table brunches, pizzas and sandwiches.

Worth a Trip 🔭

Explore the Happiest Place on Earth at Disneyland® Resort

Mickey is one lucky mouse. Walt Disney's most famous creation and a multimedia juggernaut, he lives in Disneyland, the 'Happiest Place on Earth,' where streets are always clean, employees – called 'cast members' – always upbeat, and a parade happens every day. Even cynics admit that since opening his home in 1955, Mickey's been a thoughtful host to millions of blissed-out visitors.

📞 714-781-4636

www.disneyland.com

1313 Harbor Blvd

1-day pass adult $104-149, child 3-9yr $96-141, 2-day pass adult/child 3-9yr $225/210

🕑 open daily, hours vary

Disneyland Park

Main Street USA

Fashioned after Walt's hometown of Marceline, Missouri, bustling Main Street USA (pictured) resembles the classic turn-of-the-20th-century, all-American town. complete with barbershop quartet, penny arcades, ice-cream shops and a steam train.

Great Moments with Mr Lincoln, a 15-minute audio-animatronic presentation on Honest Abe, sits inside the fascinating **Disneyland Story** exhibit, while kids love seeing early Disney cartoons like *Steamboat Willie* inside **Main Street Cinema**. Main Street ends in the **Central Plaza**, lorded over by **Sleeping Beauty Castle**, featured on the Disney logo.

Star Wars: Galaxy's Edge

Inside Disneyland's newest and largest 'land' (14 acres), the top-billed **Millennium Falcon: Smugglers Run** puts you in the cockpit of the 'fastest hunk of junk in the galaxy' on an exhilarating blast-off through hyperspace. In **Star Wars: Rise of the Resistance**, you and other 'members of the Resistance' are captured by fearsome storm troopers and must escape from a Star Destroyer.

Nearby are opportunities to make your own lightsaber or droid, or drink adult beverages or blue milk at **Oga's Cantina**, modeled after the *Star Wars* bar.

Tomorrowland

The 1950s imagineers' vision of the future is now highlighted by **Space Mountain**, one of the USA's best roller coasters, hurtling you into complete darkness at frightening speed. *Star Wars*–themed attractions (separate from Star Wars: Galaxy's Edge) include **Star Wars Launch Bay**, showing movie props and memorabilia, and **Star Tours**, which clamps you into a Starspeeder shuttle for a wild, 3D ride through the desert canyons of Tatooine.

★ Top Tips

○ Disneyland® Resort has three main areas: Disneyland Park and Disney California Adventure theme parks and outdoor pedestrian mall Downtown Disney.

○ Download the Disneyland app to check opening hours, buy admission tickets and make FASTPASS and dining reservations.

✕ Take a Break

There's no shortage of restaurants inside the resort; Downtown Disney offers dining for before, during or after your visit. Get your hand stamped and retain your ticket for re-entry to the parks.

★ Getting There

🚌 Anaheim is 25 miles southeast of Downtown LA on the I-5 Fwy.

🚃 Amtrak or Metrolink trains stop at Anaheim's ARTIC transit center, a short taxi or shuttle ride to Disneyland.

For retro high-tech, the **monorail** glides from Downtown Disney to its stop in Tomorrowland. Kiddies will want to shoot laser beams on **Buzz Lightyear Astro Blaster** and drive their own miniature cars in the classic **Autopia** ride. Then jump aboard the **Finding Nemo Submarine Voyage** to look for the world's most famous clownfish.

Fantasyland
Though it's filled with characters of classic children's stories, Fantasyland's best known for '**it's a small world**,' a boat ride past hundreds of audio-animatronic children from a world of cultures all singing an ear-worm of a theme song. Another classic, the **Matterhorn Bobsleds**, is a steel-frame roller coaster. **Mr Toad's Wild Ride** is a loopy jaunt in an open-air jalopy through London.

Younger kids love whirling around the **Mad Tea Party** teacup ride and **King Arthur Carrousel**, then cavorting with characters in nearby **Mickey's Toontown**.

Frontierland
This Disney 'land' is a salute to old Americana: the Mississippi-style paddle-wheel **Mark Twain Riverboat**, the 18th-century replica **Sailing Ship Columbia**, a rip-roarin' Old West town with a shooting gallery and the **Big Thunder Mountain Railroad**, a mining-themed roller coaster. Nearby is **Pirate's Lair on Tom Sawyer Island**.

New Orleans Square
Honoring Walt's favorite city, New Orleans Square has all the charm of the French Quarter but none of the marauding drunks. **Pirates of the**

Resort entrance

FastPass

Lines for Disneyland® Resort rides and attractions can be long, but the FastPass system can significantly cut your wait times.

○ Walk up to a FastPass ticket machine – located near attraction entrances – and insert your park entrance ticket or annual passport. You'll receive a slip of paper showing the 'return time' for boarding.

○ Show up within the window of time on the ticket and join the ride's FastPass line. There'll still be a wait, but it's shorter (typically 15 minutes or less). Hang on to your FastPass ticket until you board the ride.

○ Before getting a FastPass, check the display above the machine, which will tell you what the 'return time' for boarding is. If it's much later in the day, or doesn't fit your schedule, a FastPass may not be worth it. Ditto if the ride's current wait time is just 15 to 30 minutes.

Caribbean is the longest ride in Disneyland (17 minutes) and provided 'inspiration' for the popular movies. Over at the **Haunted Mansion**, 999 'happy haunts' – spirits, goblins, shades and ghosts – appear and evanesce while you ride in a cocoon-like 'Doom Buggy.'

Adventureland
Loosely deriving its jungle theme from Southeast Asia and Africa, Adventureland has a number of attractions, but the hands-down highlight is the safari-style **Indiana Jones Adventure**. Nearby, little ones love climbing the stairways of **Tarzan's Treehouse**. Cool down on the **Jungle Cruise**, viewing exotic audio-animatronic animals. The classic **Enchanted Tiki Room** features carvings of Hawaiian gods and goddesses and a campy show of singing, dancing audio-animatronic birds and flowers.

Disney California Adventure

Across the plaza from Disneyland, Disney California Adventure (DCA) is an ode to California's geography, history and culture – a sanitized, G-rated version at least. Opened in 2001, DCA covers more acres than Disneyland, feels less crowded and has more modern rides and attractions.

Hollywood Land
California's biggest factory of dreams is presented here in miniature, with soundstages, movable props and a studio store. **Guardians of the Galaxy – Mission: BREAKOUT!** is the newest thrill ride, a tower with drops of 130ft through the elevator shaft. The less adventurous can navigate a taxicab through 'Monstropolis' on the **Monsters, Inc: Mike & Sulley to the Rescue!** ride, and there's a one-hour live stage version of *Frozen* at the **Hyperion Theater**.

Fireworks, Parades & Shows

There's some kind of parade daily in Disneyland and DCA, with floats gliding down Disneyland's Main Street USA accompanied by favorite Disney tunes and costumed characters. Parades change seasonally and annually, but don't miss Disneyland's 10-minute nighttime 'dance party' **Mickey's Mix Magic** or DCA's premier show, the 22-minute **World of Color**.

Grizzly Peak

Grizzly Peak is DCA's salute to California's natural and human achievements. Its main attraction, **Soarin' Around the World**, is a virtual hang-gliding ride using Omnimax technology that 'flies' you over famous landmarks with a breeze in your hair and Californian aromas in your nostrils.

Grizzly River Run takes you 'rafting' down a faux Sierra Nevada river – you will get wet, so come when it's warm. While fake flat-hatted park rangers look on, kids can tackle the **Redwood Creek Challenge Trail**, with its 'Big Sir' redwoods, wooden towers and lookouts, rock slide and climbing traverses.

Cars Land

This land gets kudos for its incredibly detailed design based on the popular Disney Pixar *Cars* movies. Top billing goes to the wacky **Radiator Springs Racers**, a race-car ride that bumps and jumps around a track painstakingly decked out like the Great American West.

Tractor-towed trailers swing their way around the 'dance floor' at **Mater's Junkyard Jamboree**, or ride inside cars choreographed to classic retro tunes at **Luigi's Rollickin' Roadsters**.

Pixar Pier

If you like carnival rides, you'll love Pixar Pier, designed to look like an amalgam of California's beachside amusement piers. The state-of-the-art **Incredicoaster** glides along a smooth-as-silk track as fast as baby Jack-Jack. Just as popular is **Toy Story Midway Mania!** – a 4-D ride where you earn points by shooting at targets while your carnival car swivels and careens through an oversize, old-fashioned game arcade. It's all overlooked by **Pixar Pal-A-Round**, a 15-story Ferris wheel where gondolas pitch and yaw in little loops as well as the big one.

Nearby are rides for all ages like **Jessie's Critter Carousel**, a *Toy Story*–themed merry-go-round, and the tamer-than-it-sounds aerial spin of the **Inside Out Emotional Whirlwind**. There's also **Goofy's Sky School** and **Silly Symphony Swings** in **Paradise Gardens Park**.

Downtown Disney District

Connecting Disneyland's parks and hotels, this open-air pedestrian mall is a triumph of marketing, bursting with opportunities to drop cash in stores, restaurants and entertainment venues.

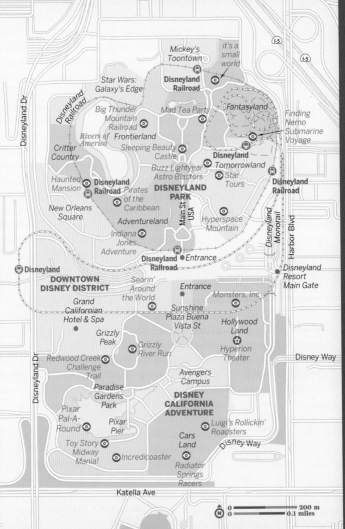

Mickey's
Toontown

it's a
small
world

Star Wars:
Galaxy's Edge

**Disneyland
Railroad**

Disneyland
Railroad

Big Thunder
Mountain
Railroad

Mad Tea Party

Fantasyland

Finding
Nemo
Submarine
Voyage

*Rivers of
America*

Frontierland

Sleeping Beauty
Castle

Disneyland

**Critter
Country**

Buzz Lightyear
Astro Blasters

Tomorrowland

Star
Tours

**Disneyland
Railroad**

Haunted
Mansion

**Disneyland
Railroad**

Pirates
of the
Caribbean

**DISNEYLAND
PARK**

New Orleans
Square

Adventureland

Main St
USA

Hyperspace
Mountain

**Disneyland
Monorail**

Harbor Blvd

Indiana
Jones
Adventure

**Disneyland
Railroad** •Entrance

Disneyland
Resort
Main Gate

Disneyland

**DOWNTOWN
DISNEY DISTRICT**

*Soarin'
Around
the World*

Entrance

Monsters, Inc

Disney Way

Grand
Californian
Hotel & Spa

Sunshine
Plaza Buena
Vista St

Hollywood
Land

Grizzly
Peak

Grizzly
River Run

Hyperion
Theater

Redwood Creek
Challenge
Trail

Avengers
Campus

**DISNEY
CALIFORNIA
ADVENTURE**

Paradise
Gardens
Park

Pixar
Pal-A-
Round

Pixar
Pier

Cars
Land

Luigi's Rollickin'
Roadsters

Disney Way

Toy Story
Midway
Mania!

Incredicoaster

Radiator
Springs
Racers

Katella Ave

0   200 m
0   0.1 miles

Survival Guide

Downtown Los Angeles SEAN PAVONE/SHUTTERSTOCK ©

Before You Go

Book Your Stay

○ LA is huge. Do your research before booking a room or house. Do you want to be within stumbling distance of hot-spot bars and clubs, near major cultural sites or by the ocean?

○ Unless you plan on driving (and spending time in traffic), find a place close to major metro or bus routes.

○ Most neighborhoods popular with visitors have hotels in just about every price range. Expect to pay between $150 and $300 per night for a midrange room.

Useful Websites

Lonely Planet (www. lonelyplanet.com/ hotels) Independent accommodations reviews, recommendations and online bookings.

HotelTonight (www. hoteltonight.com) California-based hotel-search app offering last-minute bookings.

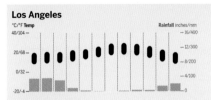

Los Angeles

°C/°F Temp
40/104 —
20/68 —
0/32 —
-20/-4 —

Rainfall inches/mm
— 16/400
— 12/300
— 8/200
— 4/100
0

When to Go

○ **Winter** (Dec–Feb) Wettest season, though temperatures are generally mild. Good hotel deals; high demand in February due to the Academy Awards.

○ **Spring** (Mar–May) Ideal time to visit. Average rainfall drops dramatically by April; decent hotel deals.

○ **Summer** (Jun–Aug) Peak tourist season; hot weather and big crowds. Outdoor concert series in full swing.

○ **Autumn** (Sep–Nov) Also ideal; warm temperatures and thinner crowds. Average rainfall remains low, especially in September.

Vrbo (www.vrbo.com) Listings include houses, apartments and B&Bs.

Best Budget

HI Los Angeles – Santa Monica (www. hilosangeles.org) Budget-friendly digs that rival facilities at properties costing many times more.

Freehand (www. freehandhotels.com/ los-angeles) Design-literate dorms in a hip Downtown hotel-hostel hybrid.

Best Midrange

NoMad Los Angeles (www.thenomadhotel. com/los-angeles) Vintage interiors and a rooftop pool in a Downtown palazzo.

Silver Lake Pool & Inn (www.palisociety.com/ hotels/silverlake) Laid-back boutique chic, steps away from hip eateries and shops.

Hotel Indigo (www. ihg.com) Svelte, plush rooms inspired by Downtown's richly textured history.

Best Top End

Sunset Tower Hotel
(www.sunsettower
hotel.com) A revamped
West Hollywood icon
rich in showbiz history.

Malibu Beach Inn
(www.malibubeach
inn.com) Coveted
art, up-close ocean
views and well-curated
interiors.

Shutters on the Beach
(www.shuttersonthe
beach.com) A New
England–style retreat in
Santa Monica.

Hollywood Roosevelt
(www.thehollywood
roosevelt.com) Holly-
wood lore lives large at
its most famous pad.

Arriving in Los Angeles

Los Angeles International Airport

LAX (LAX; www.flylax.
com; 1 World Way) is the
city's main gateway,
with nine terminals
including **Tom Brad-
ley International
Terminal**, the hub for
most international air
carriers.

○ Terminals are linked by
the free LAX Shuttle A,
leaving from the lower
(arrivals) level of each
terminal, although this is
expected to be replaced
by an elevated railway
in 2023. Hotel and car-
rental shuttles stop here
as well. A free minibus for
travelers with disabilities
can be ordered by calling
☏ 310-646-6402.

○ Cabs and ride-sharing
vehicles (including Lyft,
Opoli and Uber) are
located at the LAX-it
(pronounced 'LA Exit')
stand, about a three-
minute walk east of Ter-
minal 1. A free, frequent
shuttle bus connects all
terminals to LAX-it.

○ **LAX FlyAway** (☏ 714-
507-1170; www.lawa.org/
FlyAway) buses travel
nonstop to Downtown's
Patsaouras Transit Plaza
at Union Station (35
minutes), and Van Nuys
(40 minutes). Fares $8
to $9.75.

○ For scheduled bus
services, catch the free
shuttle bus (labeled
'Lot South/City Bus
Center') from the airport
terminals to the LAX
City Bus Center. From
here, local buses serve
all of LA County. For
Santa Monica or Venice,
change to the Santa

Monica **Big Blue Bus**
(☏ 310-451-5444; www.
bigbluebus.com) Line 3 or
Rapid 3 ($1.25). If you're
headed for Culver City,
catch **Culver City Bus**
(☏ 310-253-6510; www.
culvercity.org/how-do-i/
find/culver-city-bus) Line
6 ($1). For Manhattan,
Hermosa or Redondo
Beaches, hop aboard
Beach Cities Transit Line
109 ($1). Trip-planning
help is available at www.
metro.net.

○ LAX rail service is currently under construc-
tion. In the meantime,
if you do want to catch
a metro train service,
take the free 'Metro C
(Green) Line' shuttle
bus from the terminals
to Aviation/LAX station
and catch the Metro
C (Green) Line light
rail. For Downtown LA,
change at Willowbrook/
Rosa Parks station to the
Metro A (Blue) Line light
rail toward 7th St/Metro
Center. The rail journey
to Downtown ($1.75)
takes about one hour.

Hollywood Burbank Airport

Some domestic flights
operated by Alaska,
American, American
Eagle, Delta, Delta

Connection, JetBlue, JSX, Southwest, Spirit and United also arrive at this **airport** (BUR, Bob Hope Airport; www.hollywoodburbankairport.com; 2627 N Hollywood Way, Burbank), convenient to Hollywood, Downtown LA or Pasadena.

Long Beach Airport

Near LA County's southern border with Orange County, the small **Long Beach Airport** (www.longbeach.gov/lgb; 4100 Donald Douglas Dr, Long Beach) is convenient for Disneyland, offering a handful of domestic routes.

Union Station

Interstate Amtrak (www.amtrak.com) trains roll into Downtown's historic **Union Station** (☎Amtrak 800-872-7245; www.unionstationla.com; 800 N Alameda St).

Greyhound Bus

The main bus terminal for **Greyhound** (☎213-629-8401; www.greyhound.com; 1716 E 7th St) is in an industrial part of Downtown, so try not to arrive after dark.

Getting Around

Public Transportation

○ Most public transportation is handled by **Metro** (☎323-466-3876; www.metro.net), which offers maps, schedules and trip-planning help through its website.

○ To ride Metro trains and buses, buy a reusable TAP card. Available from TAP vending machines at Metro stations with a $2 surcharge, the cards allow you to add a preset cash value or day passes. The regular base fare is $1.75 per boarding, or $7/25 for a day/week pass with unlimited rides. Both single-trip tickets and TAP cards loaded with a day pass are available on Metro buses (ensure you have the exact change). When using a TAP card, tap the card against the sensor at station entrances and aboard buses.

○ TAP cards are accepted on DASH and municipal bus services and can be reloaded at vending machines or online on the TAP website (www.taptogo.net).

Metro Rail

The Metro Rail network consists of two subway lines, four light-rail lines and two express bus lines. Six lines converge in Downtown LA. The most useful lines for visitors are:

A Line (Blue) Light-rail line running from Downtown to Long Beach; connects with the B, D and E Lines at 7th St/Metro Center station and the C Line at Willowbrook/Rosa Parks station.

B Line (Red) The most useful for visitors. A subway linking Downtown's Union Station to North Hollywood (San Fernando Valley) via central Hollywood and Universal City.

D Line (Purple) Subway line between Downtown LA, Westlake and Koreatown. The line's extension will see it reach Beverly Hills in 2023, Century City in 2025 and Westwood in 2027.

E Line (Expo) Light-rail line linking USC and

Exposition Park with Culver City and Santa Monica to the west and Downtown LA to the northeast, where it connects with the B and D Lines at 7th St/Metro Center station.

L Line (Gold) Light-rail line running from East LA to Little Tokyo/Arts District, Chinatown and Pasadena via Union Station, Mt Washington and Highland Park; connects with the B and D Lines at Union Station.

Most lines run from around 4am or 5am to around 1am Sunday to Thursday and until around 2:30am on Friday and Saturday nights. Frequency ranges from up to every five minutes in rush hour to every 10 to 20 minutes at other times. See www.metro.net for schedules.

Metro Buses

Metro operates about 200 bus lines across the city and offers three types of bus services:

Metro Local buses (painted orange) Make frequent stops along major thoroughfares throughout the city.

Metro Rapid buses (painted red) Stop less frequently and have special sensors that keep traffic lights green when a bus approaches.

Metro Express buses (painted blue) Commuter-oriented buses that connect communities with Downtown LA and other business districts and usually travel via the city's freeways.

Municipal Buses

○ Santa Monica–based **Big Blue Bus** (☏310-451-5444; www.bigbluebus.com) serves much of western LA, including Santa Monica, Venice and Westwood. Its weekday express bus 10 runs from Santa Monica to Downtown ($2.50, one hour).

○ The **Culver City Bus** (☏310-253-6510; www.culvercity.org/how-do-i/find/culver-city-bus) runs services throughout Culver City and the Westside.

○ Long Beach and surrounding communities are served by **Long Beach Transit** (☏562-591-2301; www.ridelbt.com; per ride $1.25).

DASH Buses

These small, clean-fuel shuttle buses, run by the LA Department of Transportation (www.ladottransit.com), operate along 30 routes serving local communities (50¢ per boarding), but only until around 6:30pm to 7pm and with limited services on weekends. Many lines connect with other DASH routes; see the website for details. Here are some of the most useful lines:

Beachwood Canyon Route Useful for close-ups of the Hollywood Sign; runs from Sunset Blvd up Vine St to Hollywood Blvd and Beachwood Dr.

Downtown Routes Five separate routes hit all the hot spots. Route A runs from Little Tokyo to City West, Route B connects Chinatown to the Financial District, Route D travels between Union Station and South Park, Route E connects City West to the Fashion District and Route F connects the Financial District to Exposition Park and USC.

Fairfax Route Makes a handy loop past the Beverly Center mall, western Melrose Ave, the Farmers Market/Grove and Museum Row.

Hollywood Route Covers Hollywood east of Highland Ave and links with the short Los Feliz Route (daily) at Franklin Ave and Vermont Ave.

Observatory/Los Feliz Route Runs from Vermont/Sunset metro station (B Line) to Griffith Observatory, running north along Vermont Ave en route and south on Hillhurst Ave on the way back.

Car & Motorcycle

○ Unless time is no factor – or money is very tight – you're going to want to spend some time behind the wheel (although this means contending with some terrible traffic). Avoid rush 'hour' (7am to 9am and 3:30pm to 6:30pm).

○ Parking at motels and cheaper hotels is usually free, while fancier ones charge anywhere from $10 to $55. Valet parking at nicer restaurants is commonplace, with rates ranging from $3.50 to $10 (plus tip).

○ The usual international car-rental agencies have branches near LAX and throughout LA; some companies rent electric or hybrid vehicles. Book your vehicle in advance for the most competitive rates.

○ For Harley rentals, go to **Bartels'** (📞310-593-9767; www.eaglerider.com/bartels-harley-davidson; 4141 Lincoln Blvd, Marina Del Rey; ⏰9am-6pm Tue-Sat, 10am-5pm Sun). Rates for a Low Rider or Sportster start from around $165 per day. Discounts are available for longer rentals.

Taxi & Rideshare

○ Because of LA's size and its traffic, getting around the city by cab will cost you.

○ Cabs are best requested over the phone, though some prowl the streets late at night, and they are always lined up at airports, train stations, bus stations and major hotels.

○ Fares are metered and vary by company. In the city of LA, taxi rates are $2.85 at flagfall plus $2.70 per mile. Cabs leaving from LAX charge a $4 airport fee.

○ Los Angeles Taxi companies include **LA City Cab** (📞888-248-9222; www.lacitycab.com) and **Beverly Hills Cab** (📞800-273-6611; www.beverlyhillscabco.com).

○ Ridesharing companies Uber and Lyft are extremely popular as they are generally cheaper than cabs and often provide better service.

Essential Information

Accessible Travel

○ Los Angeles is generally well equipped for travelers with disabilities.

○ All transit companies in the LA metro area offer wheelchair-accessible services and travel discounts for travelers with disabilities. Major car-rental companies can usually supply hand-controlled vehicles with one or two days' notice.

○ Telephone companies provide free relay operators (dial 📞711) for the hearing impaired.

○ Many banks provide ATM info in braille.

o For more information, download Lonely Planet's free Accessible Travel guide from https://shop.lonelyplanet.com/categories/accessible-travel.

o Other useful resources include **A Wheelchair Rider's Guide to the California Coast** (www.wheelingcalscoast.org), the **Guide to Accessibility in Los Angeles** (www.discoverlosangeles.com) and the **Society for Accessible Travel & Hospitality** (☏ 212-447-7284; www.sath.org).

Business Hours

Banks 9:30am–4pm Monday to Friday, some 9am–2pm Saturday

Bars 4pm–2am daily

Post offices 9am–5pm Monday to Friday, some 9am–1pm or 3pm Saturday

Restaurants 7:30am–10:30am, 11am–3pm & 5:30pm–10pm daily, some later Friday and Saturday

Shops 10am–6pm or 7pm Monday to Saturday, noon–6pm Sunday (malls open later, usually 9pm or 10pm)

Supermarkets 7am–10pm daily

Electricity

Type A
120V/60Hz

Type B
120V/60Hz

Emergency & Important Numbers

Ambulance, fire or police ☏ 911

Country code ☏ 1

International dialing code ☏ 011

Operator ☏ 0

Directory assistance ☏ 411

Money

Most people don't carry large amounts of cash for everyday use, relying instead on credit and debit cards. Some businesses refuse to accept bills over $20.

ATMs

o ATMs are available 24/7 at most banks, shopping malls, airports and grocery stores.

o Expect a minimum surcharge of around $3 per transaction, in addition to any fees charged by your home bank.

o Withdrawing cash from an ATM using a credit card usually incurs a hefty fee and high interest rates; contact your credit-card company for details and a PIN.

Credit Cards

○ Major credit cards are almost universally accepted. In fact, it's almost impossible to rent a car, book a hotel room or buy tickets over the phone without one.

Taxes & Refunds

○ The California state sales tax of 7.25% is added to the price of most goods and services. Local city sales taxes may add up to 2.75% more.

○ No refunds of sales or lodging taxes are available for visitors.

Tipping

Airport skycaps & hotel bellhops $2 or $3 per bag, minimum $5 per cart.

Bartenders 15% to 20% per round, minimum $2 per drink.

Concierges Nothing for simple information; up to $20 for securing last-minute restaurant reservations, sold-out show tickets etc.

Housekeeping staff $2 to $5 daily, left under the card provided; more if you're messy.

Parking valets At least $2 when handed back your car keys.

Restaurant servers & room service 18% to 20%, unless a gratuity is already charged (common for groups of six or more).

Taxi drivers 10% to 15% of fare, rounded up to the next dollar.

Public Holidays

On the following national holidays, banks, schools and government offices (including post offices) close, and transportation, museums and other services operate on a Sunday schedule. Holidays falling on a weekend are usually observed the following Monday.

New Year's Day January 1

Martin Luther King Jr Day Third Monday in January

Presidents' Day Third Monday in February

Good Friday Friday before Easter (March/April)

Memorial Day Last Monday in May

Independence Day July 4

Labor Day First Monday in September

Columbus Day Second Monday in October

Veterans Day November 11

Thanksgiving Day Fourth Thursday in November

Christmas Day December 25

Safe Travel

Los Angeles is a reasonably safe place to visit. The greatest danger is posed by car accidents (buckle up – it's the law).

Earthquakes happen all the time, but most are so tiny they are detectable only by sensitive seismological instruments. If you are caught in a serious shaker:

○ If indoors, get under a sturdy desk or table and cover your head and neck with your arms. If in bed in the dark, stay in bed and cover your head and neck with a pillow.

○ Stay clear of windows, mirrors or anything that might fall.

○ Don't head for elevators and never go running into the street.

○ If outdoors, get away from buildings, trees and power lines.

• If driving, pull over to the side of the road away from bridges, overpasses and power lines.

• If you're on a sidewalk near buildings, duck into a doorway to protect yourself from falling bricks, glass and debris.

• Prepare for aftershocks. Turn on the radio and listen for bulletins.

COVID-19

• COVID-19 travel protocols are subject to change. For updated information on requirements for travel to/within the US, visit the CDC website (www.cdc.gov/coronavirus) and www.canitravel.net.

• Current COVID-19 protocols for Los Angeles County can be found at http://publichealth.lacounty.gov. Some venues may require proof of vaccination to enter.

Telephone Services

• US phone numbers consist of a three-digit area code followed by a seven-digit local number. In Greater Los Angeles, dial 🖉1 before all digits.

• You'll need a multiband LTE, GSM or UMTS phone to make calls in the USA. Popping in a US prepaid rechargeable SIM card is usually cheaper than using your network.

• SIM cards are sold at telecommunications and electronics stores. These stores also sell inexpensive prepaid phones, including some airtime.

Tourist Information

Discover Los Angeles Visitor Information Center (Map p38, B3; 6801 Hollywood Blvd; ⏱9am-10pm Mon-Sat, 10am-7pm Sun; 📶) The main tourist office for Los Angeles, located in Hollywood. Maps, brochures and lodging information, plus tickets to attractions. The **Union Station** (www.discoverlosangeles.com; Union Station, 800 N Alameda St; ⏱9am-5pm) branch in Downtown LA is also useful.

Beverly Hills Visitors Center (🖉310-248-1015; www.lovebeverlyhills.com; 9400 S Santa Monica Blvd; ⏱9am-5pm Mon-Fri, 10am-5pm Sat & Sun; 📶)

Santa Monica Visitor Information Center (🖉800-544-5319; www.santamonica.com; 2427 Main St; ⏱11am-4pm Wed-Sun)

Visit West Hollywood (Map p78, C3; 🖉800-368-6020, 310-289-2525; www.visitwesthollywood.com; 1017 N La Cienega Blvd, Ste 400, West Hollywood; ⏱9am-5pm Mon-Fri; 📶)

Responsible Travel

• Where possible, get from A to B using buses or the metro; the latter is a great way of avoiding LA's notorious traffic.

• If you do drive, go easy on the air-conditioning. Open the window and catch a breeze instead.

• Shop ethically and sustainably. Ditch major chains for smaller independent shops showcasing local artists, artisans and designers.

• Stock up at LA farmers markets (don't forget your reusable bag!) and choose eateries that champion seasonality, sustainability and regional produce.

• You'll find numerous volunteering opportunities at www.laworks.com.

Behind the Scenes

Send Us Your Feedback

We love to hear from travelers – your comments help make our books better. We read every word, and we guarantee that your feedback goes straight to the authors. Visit **lonelyplanet.com/contact** to submit your updates and suggestions.

Note: We may edit, reproduce and incorporate your comments in Lonely Planet products such as guidebooks, websites and digital products, so let us know if you don't want your comments reproduced or your name acknowledged. For a copy of our privacy policy visit lonelyplanet.com/privacy.

Cristian's Thanks

Muchas gracias to the Angelenos who generously shared their passion for LA, especially Daphne Barahona and Nathan Alexander, Mimi Do, Jen Berry, Sara Ventiera, Ty Holliman and Mario Ramone, Seana Corcoran, Michael Darling and Bradley Tuck. Thanks also to my sister Barbara Bonetto, *cumpà* Chris Toomey and nephews Joshua and James, for helping make this trip extra special. At Lonely Planet, much gratitude to Grace Dobell for the commission.

Andrew's Thanks

Thanks to all of the good folks of LA who helped me to show off the best of my home region. Thanks to all in-house for their hard work, patience and good cheer.

Acknowledgements

Cover image: Hollywood Blvd, Sean Pavone/Alamy Stock Photo ©

Back cover photograph: Santa Monica beach, Melpomene/Shutterstock ©

Photographs pp30–1 (from left): Natalia Macheda; Just Another Photographer; Debbie Ann Powell; Beketoff; LnP images/Shutterstock ©

This Book

This 6th edition of Lonely Planet's *Pocket Los Angeles* guidebook was researched and written by Cristian Bonetto and Andrew Bender. The previous edition was also written by Cristian and Andrew, and the 4th edition was written by Adam Skolnick. This guidebook was produced by the following:

Senior Product Editors Sasha Drew, Grace Dobell, Daniel Bolger

Cartographers Julie Sheridan, Rachel Imeson

Product Editors James Appleton, Saralinda Turner

Book Designers Nicolas D'Hoedt, Clara Monitto

Assisting Editors Gemma Graham, Victoria Harrison, Kate James, Kate Kiely

Cover Researchers Gwen Cotter, Naomi Parker

Thanks to Ronan Abayawickrema, Karen Henderson, Sonia Kapoor, Alison Lyall, Jennifer Sly, Lara Stoute

Index

See also separate subindexes for:
- ⊗ **Eating p189**
- ⊙ **Drinking p190**
- ☆ **Entertainment p191**
- ⊕ **Shopping p191**

Sights 000
Map Pages **000**